I Ruth:

Autobiography of a Marriage

"I Ruth take thee James
to my wedded husband . . ."

I Ruth: WITHDRAWN

Autobiography of a Marriage

The Self-Told Story of the Woman Who Married
the Great Lincoln Scholar, James G. Randall,
and Through Her Interest in His Work
Became a Lincoln Author Herself

by Ruth Painter Randall

BOSTON LITTLE, BROWN AND COMPANY TORONTO

Published simultaneously in Canada
by Little, Brown & Company (Canada) Limited

PRINTED IN THE UNITED STATES OF AMERICA

*This book is for Jim
whose personality I have tried to capture
in its pages*

Acknowledgments

My first expression of gratitude, I think, should go to the beneficent providence which preserved an amazingly complete body of intimate material for this book. There were a number of times when parts of it were in jeopardy and might so easily have been lost. For instance, I had kept diaries from age fourteen until three years after my marriage, and at one time, thinking there was no point to keeping them, I definitely decided to destroy them. But somehow I never got around to doing it.

It was certainly providential that on a visit to my oldest sister in Cleveland, I happened to see a large drawer full of letters. When I asked what they were, my sister answered that they were old letters written by our father and mother and that she was going to burn them. "Oh, give them to me," I said. "I would like to read them sometime." These letters proved to be real treasure when I came to write of my childhood.

Some of the letters belonging to my husband and me were lost in the confusion of several moves and I thought our letters written during our long engagement were gone. Yet, when I came to rounding up my source material for this book, I discovered that these letters had survived all moves. My husband, Jim, had carefully packed them in a box and I found them safe in a basement storeroom.

The most important source for this book is the collection of thirty diaries which Jim kept from the beginning of 1924 up to three days before his death in 1953. With my own diaries added to these, I have had, with the exception of the three years between 1920 and 1924, an account of each day from the time Jim and I first met until the week of his death. Since I quote frequently from his diaries, this book is, in a double sense, autobiographical.

For every stage of my story somehow the right papers turned up. Even for the chapter about our cat Bambi I found I had the letters which Bambi (with my secretarial help), supposedly wrote my father and mother telling them all the family news from his catly viewpoint. I have good reason to be grateful to providence for the preservation of all this invaluable material for an autobiography.

My husband's sisters, Alice Randall Jenney and Mary Randall Enlow, have contributed much in telling me about his childhood. Also, conversations with my sister Laura Painter George have filled in details of many incidents which happened when we were children together.

Since I have found it difficult to write so personal a

narrative as this book, the warm interest of friends has meant a great deal to me. To my great profit Alice Harnish has taken time out from a very busy life to serve as a touchstone, letting me read each chapter to her as it was written. It has been extremely helpful to me to talk over various problems with a well-known author and dear friend, Rebecca Caudill Ayars. Another cherished adviser has been Margaret Johnson who belongs to that lively young group of aspiring writers with whom I often meet, the Creative Writing Group of the American Association of University Women. Constance Geist, to whom I read two or three of the early chapters, has paid a number of long distance telephone bills to learn the details of the progress of my manuscript. My typist, Helen Folk, who has the nice gift of enthusiasm, has constantly given me encouragement. Martin P. Claussen, once a graduate student of my husband's, thoughtfully prepared a folder of hard-to-get material in Washington.

I wish to express my appreciation to the following: to the Columbia Broadcasting System's "CBS News Photo," for permission to use one of their photographs which includes my husband; to the *Saturday Review* for permission to reprint two of my contributions to their magazine, "We Have Had a Book" and "Home Economics," and also to reproduce the drawing which was on the cover of the *Saturday Review* November 17, 1945; to Frances O'Brien, the artist, for the use of this same drawing; to Dodd, Mead for permission to quote a passage from the preface of my husband's *Lincoln the Liberal Statesman;* to Wayne C. Temple, editor of the

Lincoln Herald, for permission to quote from my article "Little Stories from the Lincoln Papers," published in the *Lincoln Herald,* and also to quote from his letter of condolence; and finally to Ned Bradford of Little, Brown for permission to quote the telegram he sent me after he read the manuscript of *Mary Lincoln: Biography of a Marriage.*

Realizing all too well how difficult it is to write one's own story objectively, I especially asked Helen Jones and Mary Rackliffe of Little, Brown to give me editorial suggestions. I am grateful to them both for complying with this request in the best possible way.

I am again deeply indebted to Helen Hart Metz for making an excellent index.

RUTH PAINTER RANDALL

Contents

I Ruth:

Autobiography of a Marriage

1.

Most Exciting Moment

At nine-thirty that evening, the telephone rang. "Come over here as quickly as you can," said Jim's voice. "I'll meet you at the door to get you past the guard."

My spirits soared. So I was to be at the great occasion after all! Jim was phoning from the Library of Congress, where at one minute after midnight (the first minute of July 26, 1947), there would occur in that historic building an event we had been looking forward to for a long, long time.

Jim, my husband, was Professor James G. Randall of the University of Illinois. He had written several volumes on his specialty, the presidency of Abraham Lincoln, and there was every reason why he should be intensely interested in what was going to happen that evening. Lincoln's presidential papers, all the letters and documents which were in his files at the White House on that dark night when he was assassinated, had been held in secrecy for eighty-two years. Lincoln's son Robert had decreed that these papers, all eight trunkfuls of them, should not be opened until twenty-one years

after his own death. Robert died on July 26, 1926, and
now the twenty-one years had passed. At long last these
valuable papers were to be brought out of their hiding
and examined by historians.

Jim had obtained leave from the University of Illinois
and we had come to Washington several weeks ahead of
the opening. We were to spend three months in an intensive study of the papers to find out what historic secrets
they might contain. Jim's research assistant Lavern
Hamand and his wife had come to Washington also to
help in the investigation.

The very fact that the papers had been withheld
added enormously to public curiosity and speculation
about them. Newspapers had been full of the coming
event. Jim, as a specialist, had been bombarded with
questions, the most frequent one being "What's in the
papers?" He had a good answer to this: with a smile he
would say he was reminded of the burlesque examination
question: "Name the undiscovered islands of the Pacific
Ocean"! We knew at least we were to have the privilege
of looking over Lincoln's shoulder, as it were, and reading his incoming mail with him. We also suspected
(correctly, as it proved) that we might find original
drafts of his speeches, with the revisions he made as he
worked over them — speeches which have become immortal.

Lincoln scholars and devotees from all over the country had been invited to a dinner in the Library of
Congress on the evening of July 25. But alas, only men
were to be guests at that dinner! I had worked with Jim

in his research for years and was as interested in Lincoln as any of them, and I longed intensely to be at that post-midnight ceremony. My spirits were low as I watched Jim start off alone about seven-fifteen. Knowing that Lavern and his wife Martha were aching to go to the big event too, I had invited them to have dinner at the Ugly Duckling and spend the evening with me in our little apartment.

We were trying to console each other when at nine-thirty that blessed telephone message came. Jim explained: "The dinner is over now and I can get you in. Several of us have arranged for our wives to join us. Bring Lavern and Martha too." I turned to their questioning faces and joyfully announced: "Come on, we are going to be in on it too!"

We almost ran the several blocks which lay between us and the Library. Jim met us at the door as he had said he would and took us into a large banquet room where about two dozen men were assembled around a long dining table. Many of them were friends of ours, and I knew all of them by reputation. I had recognized Carl Sandburg's booming laugh even before we came in the door. After we were seated along the wall, I found I was near Carl, who got up and came over to speak to me.

There was an electric excitement in the air and high good humor. The men were making short, witty speeches, exchanging shop talk and repartee, and occasionally moving around, passing the time until the magic hour of midnight approached. There was no lack of a congenial topic: these men were drawn together by their

intense interest in Abraham Lincoln. One of them remarked: "Not since that morning in the Peterson
House* have so many men who love Lincoln been
gathered together in one room."

Shortly before twelve the word came to move. The
Lincoln Papers are not in the main building of the
Library of Congress, the domed structure with which all
are familiar, but across the street in the Library Annex. I
shall never forget that eerie walk in the sultry darkness.
There had been so much talk of people and events in the
1860's that I could almost feel the spirits of the past
flying around us. Midnight was at hand:

> . . . *the very witching time of night,*
> *When churchyards yawn* . . .

Inside the marble Annex we assembled in the Manuscripts Division on the third floor, where we stood
facing the huge safe that held the papers. By this time we
had been joined by newspaper, radio, and movie men
with their big floodlights and cameras.

There was a hush and then dead silence. Midnight
struck. The Librarian of Congress, Luther Evans, began
to intone the deed of gift. It sounded like what it really
was, a voice from the tomb: "I, Robert Todd Lincoln
. . . sole surviving child of Abraham Lincoln and the
absolute owner of all of the letters, manuscripts, [and]
documents . . . left by my father . . . do hereby give
the same in perpetuity to the United States of America."

At the safe Percy Powell of the Library twirled the

---

* The house in which Lincoln died.

knob to work the combination. The door swung slowly open. The papers concealed for eighty-two years were drawn forth.

The almost unbearable suspense was suddenly broken. There began the whir and clicking of the many cameras, and muttered remarks such as "Down in front, you're in the way of my picture." The spooky atmosphere vanished in feverish activity. All present were milling and buzzing around the hundred and ninety-four blue buckram folios with red leather labels in which the papers had been placed.

In the crowding and confusion I soon lost sight of Jim. He was off somewhere being interviewed for a radio broadcast. A charming young man named John Daly (later of *What's My Line*) asked him how he felt about the opening of these papers. Jim quoted two lines from the poet Keats:

> *Then felt I like some watcher of the skies*
> *When a new planet swims into his ken . . .*

No one was to get any sleep that night. At 3:30 A.M. Jim was bending over one of the big volumes in preparation for a CBS broadcast which he, Paul Angle, Jay Monaghan, and Carl Sandburg were to give that afternoon. Another familiar and distinguished TV personality, Eric Sevareid, had a part in the production. One excitement followed another on that memorable July 26.

Sometimes one is asked, "What has been the most exciting moment in your life?" I think perhaps the opening of the Lincoln Papers was my most exciting moment. How had it all come about? What had been the links in the chain of my life which had brought me to this experience? When I was a small child in Virginia, the name Abraham Lincoln had meant no more to me than any other name in the list of United States Presidents which I was supposed to learn.

The time has come to leave that exciting post-midnight scene in the nation's capital and take up my story at its beginning. To do this requires a journey in time and space to a quiet little town in Virginia about two hundred miles southwest of Washington. The name of that town suggests the change in atmosphere; it was Salem, which means peace. I must go back to a big rambling white house in Salem and get myself born.

2.

Big Family:
"A Little Republic, Usually Verging on Anarchy"

Lights had burned in the windows of a downstairs bedroom of that house during the night of October 31. Two lines from the song "Dixie" may well apply to my birth:

> *In Dixie Land whar I was born in,*
> *Early on one frosty mornin'* —

for I made my first appearance at 5 A.M. on November 1. Since the night before had been Halloween, my oldest sister used to tease me by saying the Halloween witches left me behind.

I was the youngest in a family of six children in which girls were very much in the majority. A boy undoubtedly would have been more welcome, as certainly five daughters to one son seemed a little one-sided. Nevertheless, there was always room for one more in our big household. When the other children returned from the home of our neighbor Mrs. Brown, where they had been sent the night before because of my impending birth, they were greatly interested in viewing the new addition to the family. My ten-year-old sister Elizabeth, feeling that some permanent record should be kept about so important an event, got her pencil, went out to the kitchen, which was in an ell of the house at the back, climbed the stairs to the "cook's room" over it, and wrote on the wall an impressive, dated announcement of my arrival!

Our house had literally grown as the family increased; that is, as baby after baby arrived, additions were built on. When I knew it, it had eleven rooms besides two room-sized halls, four porches, and a large third-story attic. Its grounds included a deep front lawn, a backyard which was the flower garden, a vegetable garden, orchard, and pasture, adding up to ten or twelve acres in all, with numerous outbuildings. There could hardly have been a nicer place in which to bring up (or, as we would have said, "raise") a large, lively family of children.

Salem was a beautiful little town in which to be born. It lay in a green valley completely surrounded by blue mountains. The sun rose over them in the morning and passed over Twelve O'Clock Knob around noon, a fact that had given the name to that picturesque peak south of the town. A line of blue or purple mountains (they were always changing color), made a vast stage for the production of spectacular sunsets in the west. The business part of Salem on Main Street, with the courthouse and a few stores, would look very quaint and old-fashioned today. We did most of our shopping in Roanoke by boarding a streetcar in front of Dillard's drugstore, whose windows containing huge glass bottles filled with colored water, red, and blue and green, I admired extravagantly as a little girl.

My earliest recollection goes back to the time when I was so small that I still slept in a crib in my father's and mother's bedroom. This meant, of course, that as soon as I awoke in the morning, I would crawl into bed with them. On this one morning which remains in my memory, my mother was already up and doubtless in the kitchen helping "Aunt Mary" with breakfast. My father, however, was still in bed, and when I climbed on it I found his bent knees under the covers created an inviting little stool just the right size for me, so I promptly sat down on it. I am sure his usual twinkle came into his eyes, for suddenly my stool, like London Bridge, was falling down and I was tumbling into the bedclothes squealing with delight over his joke. When I jumped up eagerly, the stool rose again and he, sleepy as he was, continued to play this newly invented game with me. It was one of his endearing traits that he would always enter into anything in which his children took an interest.

The bedroom of my parents, which we called "Mama's room," was downstairs. It also served as the family sitting room, the parlor being used only on special occasions or when we had callers.

I soon graduated from the crib on the first floor to sleeping in an upstairs bedroom with one of my sisters. I like to remember the secure and happy feeling with which I would wake up in the morning. The room would be darkened but the good air which blew down from our pine-covered mountains would be coming in through the slats of the shutters. They were stout wooden shutters which were always closed and securely fastened on all our windows at night.

Perhaps the first sound I would hear on waking would be a distant rooster's crowing from our chicken house, which stood far back in the rear of our home. It was a sound I always loved to hear, perhaps because it was associated in my mind with that early morning coziness. I knew that out in the kitchen Aunt Mary would be preparing breakfast. (Well-brought-up children in the South were taught to call older colored people Uncle or Aunt.) My sister still slept beside me. Before long now my mother's voice would call from the foot of the stairs: "It's going on eight o'clock, children," and I would jump out of bed to unfasten the shutters and open them on a new day. By this time there would be shutter-opening and stirrings in the other three upstairs bed-rooms. Young voices began to chatter as we hastily put on our clothes and raced noisily down the stairs to enter the dining room.

We gathered around the table, which was necessarily a long one. At one end my father would be serving the

My Parents and My Birthplace

The camera caught my father's characteristic twinkle. This big house in which I grew up was white with green shutters.

plates with the main dish, bacon and eggs, or sausage, and often fried chicken, all served with grits. Aunt Mary would be bringing in some kind of hot bread, pancakes perhaps, which we called "batter cakes," or corn muffins made with water-ground cornmeal, or hot biscuits, and sometimes waffles baked in a large waffle iron over a wood fire in the big kitchen cookstove.

Now while the family is assembled is a good time to look around the table and find out what each individual was like: My father, who always wrote his name as F. V. N. Painter, was a professor at Roanoke College, whose campus was only about two blocks from our home on High Street. By the time I was born, he had written books on English and American literature which were used in high schools and colleges over the country. He had a pleasant scholarly face with gray eyes that were quick to light up with a twinkle, for his was a keen sense of humor and he was full of fun. Though his hair had been a medium brown before it was sprinkled with gray, his mustache and Vandyke beard were auburn. He loved people and his gentle and genuinely interested manner drew them to him.

As a very little girl I considered his mustache and beard the handsomest adornments in the world. Once around this time I said to my pretty mother, as I affectionately stroked her cheek: "Mama, why aren't you beautiful like my beautiful Papa?" She made it clear that she did not appreciate this question, but the truth was that I was regretting the fact she did not have a mustache and beard!

my mother. I have two picture-clear recollections of Aunt Mary. In one of them I was sitting on her lap in our big kitchen and lovingly reaching up to pat her brown cheeks. In the other I was looking down, in distress and awe, on her calm, still face in her coffin, her hands crossed on her breast. It was my first awareness of death.

After Aunt Mary came a succession of hired "cooks," as we called them. It was a new order of things which showed how the way of living into which I was born was rapidly ceasing to exist.

There is a long list of personalities who were unmistakably members of our family, our pets. If ever there was a household which had a passionate love of animals, it was ours. When we gathered together in the dining room there was sure to be a cat or dog present, quietly collecting tidbits which were slipped to him under the table.

The pets I remember best from this early period were Gladstone and Fritzie. We did not choose Gladstone; he chose us. One morning, shortly after shutter-opening time, my brother, who had dressed ahead of the rest of us and gone downstairs, discovered a large Newfoundland dog sitting on the kitchen porch. The big fellow at once courteously offered his paw for a handshake. Boy's shouts of delight soon brought the rest of us, some half dressed, and the dog offered a paw to each in turn. Then my mother appeared, to have a paw offered to her, and she of course set about getting a plate of food for the visitor. In the general excitement, we gradually realized what my brother kept saying: "He's my dog! I have been praying for a dog and here he is! Can I keep him?"

Finally my father appeared, and the dog, recognizing that here was an important member of the family, sat up on his haunches and offered both front paws to the man of the house. That did it! My father accepted the double handshake, patted the dog on the head, and said, "Yes, Boy, if we cannot find the owner, you can keep him."

The owner proved to be a farmer living out in the country. He said the dog was no good to him as he kept running away. I suspect that my father offered an acceptable price for the dog; at all events he became ours with the former owner's consent. It developed that the farmer had no children and the dog loved children. Just what sort of survey he had made before selecting us for his family we could not know, but certainly no diplomat could have managed his entry into our household more skillfully. In consideration of his dignity we named him Gladstone, and he watched faithfully over all of us for years. Never once did he run away.

Fritzie was a beautifully marked gray cat with an amiable disposition. He would let me dress him in baby clothes and wheel him around in my doll buggy. One day our sister Margaret, who had just acquired a new camera, stopped Boy and me, as we played together in the front yard, to take a picture of us. I insisted that Fritzie should be in the picture and posed him on the stump of the buckeye tree which had recently been cut down. Boy wanted his little shotgun to have its picture taken too. So Margaret snapped the camera and thus preserved the image of us both as we were in that one moment of our childhood.

A little black cat named Satan I remember only because he caused me one of my early embarrassing moments. Satan was in the front yard and I wanted to call him to be fed. But on the front porch sat my father with a visiting minister. What would that preacher think if he heard me calling "Satan, Satan!" Suddenly a solution of the problem came to me. I would call "Satin, Satin!" I figured that the cat would not know the difference and the minister would be spared a shock!

The front porch and front yard figured largely in our lives in warm weather. The porch, our outdoor sitting room, had a railing whose top was wide enough for us children to sit on and dangle our legs. It looked out over the long smooth stretch of lawn with its half-dozen trees which made an ideal playground. A wrought-iron fence ran along the street side of this front yard with white picket fences at either side, and here with the neighbor children in the summer evenings we played everything from hide-and-seek to baseball.

The huge cork elm tree which stood near the front porch was the home base for hide-and-seek. I can still feel how rough its bark was when I was "it" and stood with closed eyes leaning my forehead against the trunk. While the others hid I would call out in singsong fashion, "Five-ten-fifteen-twenty," and so on up to one hundred. Then I would chant, "Bushel of wheat, bushel of rye, all not ready holler 'I.'" If there were answering I's, I would have to count again to one hundred. My father and mother would probably be sitting on the front porch, perhaps with neighbors who had dropped in, chatting against the background of children's voices.

In the winter evenings we would gather in "Mama's room," where often there would be a fire in the fireplace. My mother might be sewing, or more likely darning our multitude of stockings. Some of the young people would be reading, or studying their lessons. This was the scene described in one of the little domestic poems which my father wrote for his own pleasure. He always liked, when his children were very small, to sing them to sleep in the evenings, and eventually my turn came. I can remember how careful he was to shade my eyes from the light, how softly he sang, and how he would explain the words of the song to me. This poem — there were two more stanzas — is entitled "Ruth."

> *When the evening lamp is shining bright,*
> *And round it sit the family band,*
> *Each one, beneath the kindly light,*
> *Pursuing the task that lies at hand, —*
>
> *Then climbs upon my waiting lap*
> *My five-year-old with curling hair,*
> *And nestles, for her evening nap,*
> *Against my cheek with face so fair.*

These are unpretentious old-fashioned verses, but they do express a feeling which has been universal through the ages, a father's joy in holding his own child. I had evidently been prepared for bed before he sang me to sleep, and later, when the others went upstairs to bed, I was carried up and tucked in. I was never put upstairs in bed alone after a certain vivid experience. The family had been reading aloud *The Hound of the Baskervilles*, and shortly after I had been tucked in upstairs I came screaming out of the bedroom crying that the Hound of the Baskervilles had put his head in the window and flicked out his tongue at me!

In such a large family, of course, there were illnesses (with quarantines for such childhood diseases as measles), accidents, and miscellaneous unpleasant surprises. In one of those evening games of hide-and-seek, Laura, running toward home base, tripped over the front yard hydrant and broke her arm. Remembering how Aunt Mary had looked in her coffin, I was agonized when I heard Laura crying and knew that there had been a hurried call for the doctor. I tried to get an answer to my frantic question, "Will she die? Will she die?" Finally one of my older sisters reassured me.

Once my brother went to death's very door with scarlet fever. Later, when he and Laura had entered their teens, came the first operation in the family. This was after Margaret had finished her work at medical college and was interning at a hospital in Detroit. Operations were much less frequent than they are today and, lacking modern techniques, were considered very dangerous. When a telegram came saying that Margaret was having an emergency operation for appendicitis, there was consternation in the family. My father and mother hastily prepared to take the first train west and circumstances left us three younger children alone in the big, creaky house on the night after they had departed.

I remember vividly how forlornly we three sat in the downstairs hall that evening after a dismal supper. We were worried about our sister, and to have both of our parents leave was like knocking down the foundations of the house. To add to our nervousness there had been a violent thunderstorm that afternoon which had put our electric lights out of order and left the house in total darkness. A single candle in the hall threw long, spooky shadows. We talked in low, subdued tones.

We were burglar-conscious because there had been several attempts to break into our house in the past. This may have had something to do with the fact that our father had taught all of us how to shoot a little twenty-two revolver. With this background Laura had developed a marked talent for hearing burglars at night. She could not possibly pass up such an appropriate occasion as this. "I hear a burglar," she whispered, sending cold chills down my back.

We huddled together while we considered what to do. Laura said we must get the pistol and shoot it out of the upstairs hall window to scare the burglar away. A few moments later a queer little procession of scared children was going up the stairs. Laura went first, clutching the revolver. Boy came close behind her, and I, carrying the candle in my trembling hand, brought up the rear. I stayed so close to Boy that the candle nearly burned a hole in the seat of his pants just in front of me on the stairs! We crouched at the window, where Laura cautiously unfastened and opened the shutters just enough to get her hand with the pistol outside. She pulled the trigger and the shot rang out.

Pandemonium broke loose. Gladstone, outdoors in the backyard, began a thunderous barking. Pigeons roosting on the ridge of the roof above came flying down past the window with a whizzing, bullet-like sound that made Laura fall back on Boy and me. We all sprawled in a heap on the floor. The noise was enough to scare off half a dozen burglars.

When the reassuring daylight came, Boy made an investigation. There were occasions when he felt it was quite a trial to live with so many sisters and their feminine notions, and this was one of them. The kitchen, one remembers, was in an ell at right angles to the house at the back. Boy reported what he had found. "That silly girl," he said disgustedly, "has shot a hole in the kitchen roof."

When I was about six years old, one day I felt sick and my throat hurt. My temperature was taken and proved to be very high. The doctor came and took a culture. Suddenly the other children were being kept out of the room and there was a quarantine sign on the front door. I had diphtheria.

I remember my fear of the long needle which administered the saving antitoxin and the weird feeling which was caused either by drugs or delirium, a feeling that time and space had opened up into a terrifying vastness. My mother, as always, nursed me carefully. She was a rather nervous little woman, but in a time of crisis she could be counted on to show a wonderful pluck and strength.

It was a desperate illness, and when it was over I was no longer the healthy child I had been. The diphtheria had caused some heart damage and I was destined to have one throat infection after another for years. It was time for me to start to the public school which the other children had attended.

But I would never go to that school.

3.

Emotional Ups and Downs in My Teens

The diphtheria delayed my going to any school for a year. The fact that it had left me in such uncertain health was undoubtedly the main reason why my parents then decided to have me taught at home. My father would select one of the best and most suitable students in his classes, a young man, and have him come to the house to give me lessons. In the end I did not attend any public school at all until I entered the preparatory department at Roanoke College. I was, so to speak, hand-educated up to this point.

My father himself kept in close touch with what I was being taught. As soon as I had learned to write he made a bargain with me: he would give me five cents for each little poem I copied for him, and he would select the poems. I was still in the stage at which I had to form each letter laboriously and by the time I had copied a verse, I knew it by heart. I suspect that by this time he knew that I was going to love all the things he did, books, writing, and languages, and he was starting my literary education. It was some years later that he told me something I have been glad to remember. We had been talking over some little problem in my studies, as we always did, and he asked me what I thought about it. When I answered he said: "I knew you would look at it that way; your mind works exactly like mine." It was my privilege to have his guidance all the way through my educational growing-up.

My older sisters had already graduated from college when I was still a small girl and we had begun to have weddings. The first naturally was that of the eldest daughter, Julia. Roanoke College, from which we would all graduate in time, seemed to have become a family institution; it was to serve as a sort of matrimonial bureau for three of us! Julia and Elizabeth both married young men who came to the college as students. All five of the Painter girls were married in what was called the College Church.

Julia married Archibald H. Throckmorton, who later became a professor of law. Their wedding was in June, when Virginia fields were white with daisies, so daisies were used in the yellow-and-white church decorations. I was in the wedding party as a little flower girl while my brother was the ring-bearer. I remember well my perky little dress of yellow organdy, my basket of flowers, and my brother's small white suit. We walked up the aisle together and in the sudden hush as we entered I heard whispered comments such as "The darlings! Oh, aren't they precious," which gave me a truly feminine satisfaction. After the ceremony, which almost overwhelmed me with its unexpected solemnity, I strewed flowers in front of the bride as she walked down the aisle on the arm of her husband.

It was the first break in the family and I sensed that my father and mother felt a little sad about the gap in the circle around the table. But we still had a substantial quorum, and a new pattern of family life would develop. As one by one the members married or went away for professional training, it became the custom for them to return to the old home place in the summers for as long a visit as they could manage with their new responsibilities.

At Elizabeth's marriage to Henry W. A. Hanson, I rather disgraced myself during the wedding reception. The solemn words of the marriage service and the impending goodbyes really did overwhelm me this time. I was supposed to ladle out the punch to the guests and I was discovered weeping over the punchbowl. Diluting the punch with salt tears was against the rules and I was promptly replaced by a dry-eyed substitute!

The fact that Julia and Elizabeth were now away from home the greater part of the time led to many family letters, some of which were preserved. This was fortunate, for in writing biography the most desirable source material is that which was written down at the time, when impressions are close-up and clear and have not become blurred or twisted in memory by the lapse of time.

My mother would write Julia reporting on us

younger children, and sometimes in reading her letters I can look through her eyes at myself when I was a girl. The following is a passage from one of these letters: "I wish you would tell me the name of some book that would be nice for Ruth's birthday present. In less than two weeks she will be ten years old. Alas, no baby in the house!" Another passage, written when I was fourteen, contains a bit of description. She had evidently been buying me some new clothes. "I am having Ruth fixed up," wrote my mother. "She is growing fast. . . . Her hat is so becoming. She is a credit to the family."

It was also when I was fourteen that I started to keep a day-by-day diary, a practice which I continued until three years after I was married. It is a strange experience to look into my own mind as it was when I was a girl, especially in this period of great change when I was constantly discovering new mental and emotional horizons. These diaries contain in detail all the events of my college years, give a complete account of a long courtship, and describe my wedding and early married life.

Reading the early diaries I am struck by certain expressions which I would not use now. Where today, for example, I would say, "I went to town after dinner," the diary says, "Went down street after supper." Dinner with us was the midday meal, usually at one o'clock, and supper a somewhat simpler meal at six in the evening. Lunch to us meant the food we took on picnics. We often used "evening" when we meant afternoon and events after supper were at night.

I can trace the signs of my growing up in the diaries.

Various Stages of My Growing-Up

Above, left, about five years old; right, about twelve. Below,
my brother and I were called from play to pose. I insisted
on having my cat Fritzie in the picture.

Early in the year which would bring my sixteenth birthday, I find this record written in the abbreviated style which I used in the diaries: "Changed way of wearing hair. Instead of tying it with a ribbon behind, I loop it on the back of my head and wear a bow of ribbon on top." I added happily that it was thought "real becoming." Hair was worn long then and when a girl reached the stage of "putting it up" on her head, she felt quite grown-up. My hair was chestnut-colored and thick, so that the loop which made the figure 8 was bulky and had to be fastened with stout bone hairpins.

That spring I was still studying at home under my father's guidance and evidently concentrating on French. There are daily entries about reading so much French and reporting to him. Often, to my delight, he would talk to me in French at the dining table, and I would try to respond, but I never learned to speak the language.

Books had become a large part of my life. It had long been the custom for my father to read aloud to the family in the winter evenings. The reading, of course, took place in "Mama's room," and when we were little, we three youngest children would pile on the bed higgledy-piggledy and sometimes go to sleep. Now that I was in my teens, however, I frequently took my turn at the reading aloud. Our literary range was a wide one, including everything from Shakespeare's plays to the latest novel.

The group around the dining table had now grown still smaller. In addition to the two married sisters, Margaret also was living away from home, having taken a position as the women's physician in a hospital for the mentally ill at Marion, Virginia. In my sixteenth year Laura and Boy would both depart, my brother to Yale for his postgraduate work in zoology, and Laura to marry Harold C. George, a geologist and mining engineer and a delightful addition to the family.

My diary gives an account of Laura's wedding. I was so ashamed of the spectacle I had made of myself by crying at Elizabeth's wedding that I was determined not to weep at Laura's, no matter how much it hurt. I remained dry-eyed through the ceremony and reception and even accompanied the newly married pair to the railroad station to see them off. The diary records: "I didn't cry until they were gone and I am so glad I was able not to. Laura was beautiful."

I missed her terribly. She was the sister nearest my age, and we had long shared a room and were very companionable. I felt desolate in my solitary bed that night after the wedding and in the days that followed. When Boy departed in September, I was the only one left to sleep in that big upstairs that had once been filled with lively young voices. Above me, on the third floor, was the attic, which indulged in blood-chilling creaks and groans in the silence of the night, as old houses often do. I locked my bedroom door and checked the fastenings of the shutters, for I was a little bit afraid as well as very lonely.

It was fortunate that in that same September I entered the preparatory department of Roanoke College. The one regrettable feature in my being taught privately had been the absence of schoolmates. Now at last I was in classes with others. For the next five years (one year in prep school and then the usual four years leading to graduation), I would be absorbed in attending Roanoke College. With monotonous regularity the diary entries say, "Went to class. Studied."

As I walked the short distance on High Street which took me to the campus, I was likely to have an unusual escort, an individual who, deservedly, had a bad reputation in the neighborhood. He had such an urge toward petty larceny that it seemed as if he had been born, or I should say hatched, with criminal tendencies. It was our pet crow. At this point I should bring the family pets up to date, especially as they meant more to me than ever after I was the only one left at home.

Jim Crow, as we called him, liked to go to the college for several reasons. One was that the college boys usually had pencils in their breast pockets and he was making a collection of pencils in one of his secret hideouts. He would alight on a boy's shoulder and make soft, ingratiating remarks in crow language, all the while sizing up the prospects for booty and getting himself into a good stance for action. The boy would be flattered by this attention from Professor Painter's crow. Jim Crow, as soon as he got into the right position, would seize the pencil from the boy's pocket and fly off with a triumphant, jeering caw.

This mischievous bird had another way of giving the college boys a surprise. The freshmen were required to wear little green caps and Jim Crow liked nothing better than to swoop silently down on one of them from behind, seize his cap, and sail off with it, leaving the freshman looking up into the sky with his mouth open. A third pleasant pastime involved teasing a professor who was teaching a class. It was great fun from the crow's viewpoint to perch on a window ledge outside the classroom and keep tapping on the glass with his beak. This was very rewarding: it resulted in hilarity for the students and complete frustration for the professor.

Jim Crow also delighted in teasing the dogs and cats. We still had Gladstone when the bird, as a mere fledgling, was added to our menagerie. The big Newfoundland was usually fed out of doors and when the plate of food was placed before him, the crow would sneak up behind him and tweak a few hairs from his tail. The dog would whirl around, which gave the quick bird a chance to grab a bite from the plate.

Yet we loved that wicked clown of a bird and he was very loyal to the family. He was careful never to peck any of us and he seemed to have a real affection for my father. When we children were small we would watch for my father to come home from his classes so that we could run to meet him. The crow soon learned to fly along with us to welcome him. By and by he took over this habit on his own. With or without us, Jim Crow would watch for my father at the proper time and fly to meet him halfway down the block. My father would crook his arm to make a landing place and talk gently to him while the bird responded with little bits of crow chat. This engaging conversation would last all the way up the street and front walk to the front door.

The roster of pets was always changing, for the one sad thing about loving pets so dearly is that they do not live long enough. After Fritzie came a long succession of interesting cat personalities. I especially remember Mr. Yellow, an honorable but high-strung feline gentleman, who always reminded me of a certain nervous professor at the college. Mr. Yellow was very jealous of his colleague, Don, a handsome gray Maltese. The trouble was that each one wanted an exclusive position as Family Cat, and they lived in a glaring state of armed truce. However, they did join forces in teaching Laura's little black dog, Cricket, not to go through a doorway ahead of them. If Cricket thoughtlessly went first, she received a swat from behind from a paw with claws in it. Being a very smart little dog, she soon got the idea and would always stand back to let those haughty felines enter first.

I sometimes say I was raised by a collie. Our Lad, or Laddie as we called him, was a prince of that princely breed. I feel a pang of longing for him whenever I watch a certain TV show, for he looked almost exactly like Lassie. We got him when Boy and I were still small and he definitely felt that we were his children and it was his duty to look after us.

Laddie took on a number of duties. There was the matter of getting the girls up in the mornings. Boy was geared for early rising but the rest of us loved that extra few minutes more in bed when sleep is so delicious.

When the call to rise was ignored, Boy would say: "Laddie, go get those lazy girls up." Never was a task performed more efficiently! Laddie would first jump on the bed, put his nose to the victim's ear and bark loudly. If this failed to bring results, the dog would then seize the covers in his teeth and pull them off. Sometimes a mighty struggle ensued, with the would-be sleeper clutching the covers tightly and the dog pulling, barking, and wagging his tail all at once. However, by the time she had disputed the matter with a big, noisy dog who jumped all over her, she was wide awake and would get out of bed in self-defense.

Sometimes, when we had callers, we would put on an act showing how protective Laddie felt toward Boy and myself. My mother would step toward us saying to the dog: "Laddie, these children have been bad and I am going to spank them." Instantly Laddie would jump in front of us and start arguing with her, meanwhile heading off any attempt on her part to reach us. He was devoted to my mother, but he seemed to be saying something like this: "Mrs. Painter, I know you are a wonderful person, but I can't let even you spank my children!"

The time came in my teens when he really protected me in a frightening situation. It happened one summer day when I was sitting on the front porch. I was alone at the house and there was no neighbor within calling distance. A rough-looking man, evidently very drunk, opened the gate and came up the front walk. He said thickly that he wanted to use the telephone. I told him it was out of order, but he started up the porch steps toward me. I stood up, terribly frightened.

Suddenly Laddie was in front of me, pushing me back while he faced the man. Baring his teeth, he began a low, ominous growling which told the intruder plainly that if he took one step more the dog would spring at his throat. I said to the man: "If you don't leave, the dog will attack you," and he backed away, and went down the walk toward the street. Laddie was quite a hero in the family after that.

At the end of my preparatory year at the college I had the special privilege which my father gave to each one of his children in turn when they were in their teens: a trip to Washington, Philadelphia, and New York. There were just the two of us and we did a thorough job of sightseeing in all three cities. In Washington we visited the Smithsonian, the Corcoran Art Gallery, the Library of Congress, and the Capitol, stopping for a while in the Senate gallery. In the evenings while we were there, we attended two plays. It was all so new and interesting to me that I was in a constant state of thrills and wonder.

In Philadelphia we stayed at the Bellevue-Stratford Hotel, which I thought "the swellest hotel in the city." In my diary for June 30 I wrote: "It feels strange to be way up here on the 12th floor of this great hotel in this great city, but then I am having lots of new experiences these days." The stay in New York included a boat trip up the Hudson to see West Point and even a trip to Coney Island. There is no doubt my father believed in a many-sided education!

That fall I was in the freshman class at Roanoke College. I took my studies quite seriously and tended to be what was called a grind. The result was that in December, after a heart examination, the doctor ordered me to quit college for a while and take a rest. I was all broken up over this decision and could not be consoled.

I still have a playful document which my father then drew up: "AGREEMENT between F. V. N. Painter, party of the first part, and Ruth Elaine Painter, party of the second part, both of the town of Salem, State of Virginia, *Witnesseth*, that whereas the party of the second part" is in danger of impairing her health "by unnecessary worry over her studies" and so on, using elaborate legal language humorously, "the said party of the second part hereby agrees to introduce a regular system in her studies as follows." What follows is a very sensible plan for devoting a certain number of hours to study and a certain amount of time to recreation and physical exercise. The document ends: "In testimony whereof we have affixed our hands and seals," and bears my father's signature after which he has drawn a little seal.

His strategy worked. Following his rules, I was able to return to college the next quarter. The diaries, however, show unhappily that all through my college years I had many severe throat infections as well as painful headaches from eyestrain. I was often very blue about it. I did not realize then what an anxiety this was to my parents. I caught a glimpse of their worry later after my graduation, when my mother wrote me that she had heard of the untimely death of one of my college classmates. "I felt so thankful," she said, "that the Lord had spared you to us."

In the same December in which I was put on sick leave, so to speak, my first publication appeared. My diary for December 21 records the following: "The *Collegian* [the college magazine] came with my first little sonnet in it. It makes me feel funny to see a little poem of mine in print." I published several so-called poems and an article or two in The *Collegian* during my years at Roanoke College, and the heavy subjects I chose for my effusions make me smile today. One was entitled "Some Uses of the Study of Poetry." There was, however, a whimsical article which was intended to be somewhat humorous. It concerned a student who, having been out late the night before celebrating a baseball victory, falls asleep in his Latin class and has a dream in which the baseball game and the Latin get very much mixed up. I signed it facetiously "O. G. Whizz."

So my college days flowed past with the usual emotional ups and downs, the thrills, disappointments, complications and discoveries that seemed all important at the time. I had dates with various beaux and enjoyed them but they involved no deeper emotion than friendship.

The summer following my sophomore year we had the fourth wedding in the family. My sister Margaret resigned her position at the hospital to marry the cashier of the First National Bank in Marion, Virginia. She later teased him by saying she gave up three hundred lunatics to specialize on one! He was a handsome and most lovable man named Thomas E. King, but nearly everyone called him Tumpus. I said of this sister what I had said of Laura at her wedding. "Margaret looked beautiful." Perhaps all happy brides do.

At the end of my junior year I attended the commencement exercises of the college only because one of the boys I had been dating was the valedictorian of his class and would speak. My diary for that day records what happened as I sat in the audience: "Without the least warning I was asked to come up on the stage and receive a gold medal for the highest general average in college." I had not even known such a medal was offered. If I recall the circumstances correctly, the gold medal was given to the college for two years only by a gentleman with whom we were not acquainted. His son received it one year and I the other. I was then (and still am) shy of platforms, and walking up on that stage was quite an ordeal. The medal, unworn and shiny, lies today in the bottom of my jewelry box.

That summer, as usual, we had to lengthen the dining table to its fullest extent for the gathering of the clan. On July 13 I recorded an unusual joy in my diary: "Every member of our original family is home now." The lonely upstairs had come alive again, and how I loved it is shown in a passage on July 21: "Such a happy jolly day with my sisters. We dressed in our kimonos and had a regular school girl time." I added that we had eaten supper that evening in picnic fashion in the backyard flower garden. The summer was one long play time with picnics, parties, friends to dinner, and expeditions into the beautiful country around us. How I hated to say goodbye at the end of it in early September, the September when I entered the senior class.

There was a new professor at the college that fall, a professor of history. In such a small college this was an event of much interest among the students. He had recently taken his doctor's degree at the University of Chicago and his students called him "Dr. Randall." Having finished my required work in history, I was not in any of his classes, but I soon learned to know him by sight. He was slightly below middle height and had a fine, sensitive face with clear-cut features, brown eyes, and dark brown hair. I heard his students say he "knew his stuff," was an interesting teacher, and was always ready to help them in any way he could.

This book is the biography of a marriage, which means it has two leading characters. The second protagonist had now arrived upon the scene. But I was not to meet him for more than two years, and in the meantime far-reaching changes were to come to us both.

4.

Enter the Leading Man, Unrecognized

On June 11, 1913, I wrote in my diary: "I graduated from my dear old college today. Lovely presents & people so nice. To Faculty reception in afternoon."

One incident at that reception remains in my memory. It should be explained that Roanoke College at that time was not coeducational, but a few local girls were allowed to attend and would receive a certificate stating that they had completed the work required for graduation. There were only three of us that year and we did not sit on the stage with the senior class. At the reception the new professor, Dr. Randall, passed by us and remarked pleasantly, "It's a shame the prettiest part of the class was not on the platform." I noticed how his face, usually serious, lighted up when he smiled.

That summer was another of happy family reunion at the big white house on High Street. In September my sister Julia and her husband, Arch Throckmorton, would have to return to Bloomington, Indiana, where he was Professor of Law. They wanted me to spend the winter with them and take graduate work in English at Indiana University. There was an excellent professor of English there, they said, Dr. Will D. Howe.

So for the first time I started toward the Middle West, which would ultimately, in fate's design for me, become my home. On the train trip my berth in the Pullman had inadequate cover and I became chilled during the night. The result was that I began my year in Bloomington with a sharp attack of my old enemy, tonsillitis, which delayed my registering for graduate work until October 7.

Late registration was an added complication in an adjustment which I found difficult enough at best. The difference between a small Southern college, where I knew practically everyone and everyone knew me, and a big Middle Western university, where I knew no one, was rather overwhelming. The whole orientation was strange to me. The other students did not even talk as I did. When I was called on in class, my Southern accent sounded strange to them. However, I found my work in English quite satisfying and Dr. Howe a most stimulating teacher. Julia and Arch had advised me to take sociology as my minor. I did not question this advice at the time, but I have since regretted I did not take American history instead.

On top of other disturbing factors I acquired a new and permanent worry early that fall. Because of my headaches Julia took me to a good oculist in Indianapolis.

It was quite a blow when he told me I had been born with small opacities in my eyes. They were like little cataracts and explained why I did not see quite as well as other people. If they did not grow, I could get along with proper glasses. All in all I was blue and homesick those first weeks in Bloomington, although Julia and Arch were generous and good to me in every way they knew.

A cheering event occurred late in November. One day when Dr. Howe's English class assembled, he announced unexpectedly that we would have a written lesson. We were to write an essay on a certain work we had been studying. I shared fully the consternation that was visible in the faces of the other students, but, after some reflection, I settled down to writing.

In a day or two Dr. Howe returned the papers. First he made a little speech about them, saying that he had been much disappointed in them and there was only one paper in the class of forty which had received an A. He continued along this line while my heart sank lower and lower. Then he handed the papers back to us as we filed past him at the end of the period. On my essay was unbelievably a large A and his written comment, "The best paper in the class." This gave me a bit more self-confidence, a quality which I needed.

By this time I was beginning to adjust to student life in a big university and was liking it. I was making many friends, attending lectures by well-known people, and going to plays and other university events. Two young instructors, new that year, were frequent visitors at the

Throckmorton home, finding Julia's generous hospitality very attractive, and I occasionally had dates with them.

All these tangible events are recorded in my diary, but what the experience that year was opening up to me mentally is better seen in the letters I was constantly writing home. I continued to take all my psychological reactions and questions to my father. Some of these questions had now become philosophical. Here is a passage from one of my father's letters in which he speaks of my "new ideas": "It will be a pleasure to me to see how you now look upon life," he wrote. "You have already discovered that no morbid view is at all adequate or satisfying."

I do not remember what particular comment of mine prompted this reply from my father: "As to yourself, no one can look back over life without seeing that many things might have been different, and possibly better for being different. No one ever has all imaginable good things. We have to strike a general average. And if you will compare your life, not with an ideal dream, but with the lives of others, you will see, I think, deep reason for gratitude. In many respects you have been greatly blessed, as indeed our whole family has been."

Perhaps it was such guidance as this that made me write him later: "I have 'kinder' made a bargain with Providence that if I do the best I can, Providence will work things out all right."

My father was, of course, paying all my expenses. I hated to ask him for money, and I find in my letters home that I had worked out a playful signal which was a financial SOS. When I needed more money, I would begin my letter "Dear 'Honey Pa' " and a check would immediately be forthcoming!

I find something else in my letters home during my first two years away from it that I am grateful to see. A child growing up naturally takes his or her parents for granted because they have always been there. Getting away from home usually gives one a better perspective. I am glad now that I expressed my affection and appreciation to my father and mother in passages like these: "Do you know my heart is always as full of love for you two as it can be and yet my love seems to be increasing. That must be a sign my heart is growing bigger!" The following passage was written on a valentine: "Valentine's Day is the day for peeping into one's own heart, and I believe I found there this morning that you two have been elected my best beloved valentines."

Another passage referred to a family story. When I was a little girl about five, I announced at the table one day that I remembered when I was born. Since this failed to make the impression I felt it deserved, I gave the circumstantial details: "An angel brought me down from heaven," I said, "and was carrying me in his arms along High Street one night. When we came to our house, I saw there was a light in Mama's room, so I said to the angel, 'Take me in here,' and he did."

This is the story referred to in a letter to my mother. I told her I had seen some old friends from Roanoke who had many nice things to say about my "dear little mother with her bright eyes and pretty face," and equally nice things to say about my father. I continued: "Well, enough was said to make me feel, as I often do, that I was very wise when I told the angel who brought me down from heaven to stop at the Painter gate! I showed unusual wisdom in one so young in selecting my parents!"

As November passed into December that fall at Bloomington, I began to look forward to going home for Christmas. "I have some chickens I am saving to fry for you," my mother wrote late in November in a letter full of living anticipation of my coming. Her letters were opening my eyes to how much she and my father missed me, the last of their children to leave home. There was no one at all now in the big upstairs and the house seemed very empty to them.

I remember well the thrills at that Christmas homecoming. When I changed trains at Cincinnati in the evening and my Pullman was called, the very name of the railroad, Norfolk and Western, seemed like that of an old friend. It was the railroad which ran by Salem and on which we always traveled. One of the simple recreations in that town had been to walk to the station, stand on the bridge over the tracks, and watch the train from New York go through. I slept happily in my berth that night on the homeward journey and when I awoke in the morning and pushed up the shade of the window, a lump came into my throat at the sight of a big blue mountain half veiled in the mists of dawn. The train was going through the mountains of West Virginia and often, as we rounded a curve, I could see the engine ahead with its busy wheels speeding me toward home. Home! There was the climax of joy when we came to the well-known station and I saw the familiar figure of my father waiting for me. I was half laughing and half crying as I ran to kiss him. And I repeated this performance when we reached the house on High Street and I saw my mother coming forward to welcome me with so much gladness in her face.

After a happy Christmas visit I returned to Indiana University to complete my graduate work there. That spring I wrote a thesis on Charles Lamb, and at the outdoor Commencement on Indiana's beautiful campus in June I received my A.M. degree.

The summer family reunion at Salem followed. In the fall Julia and Arch moved to Cleveland, where he had accepted a position as professor of law at Western Reserve University. They were very generous to me and seemed to think by this time I half belonged to them. They wanted me to spend the winter with them again and take further graduate work at Western Reserve. This was decided upon.

Graduate work at Western Reserve at that time did not prove as fruitful as the catalog had led us to suppose. But I did find one rewarding course in American history with Dr. E. J. Benton, with whom I formed a warm and lasting friendship. The winter was a rich one in other ways. There were all the attractions offered by a big city in drama, music, lectures, and meeting interesting people. I did some work in the libraries to help my father, who was revising his *Introduction to American Literature.* Letters passed constantly between us. One of them in the spring brought me that special sadness which comes to people who love their pets perhaps too dearly. Our collie, Laddie, had died. In writing me about this, my father made a comment which expressed my own feeling: "Have dogs souls? . . . If Lad's spirit has not survived, then something beautiful in affection, unselfishness, and loyalty has been lost to the universe."

After the usual gathering of the clan that summer, Arch and Julia wanted me to return with them to Cleveland. But I knew now that I could not go on with graduate studies there, and it seemed to me I was needed more at home. My parents had both been forty at the time I was born and I realized they were no longer young. In a letter I had written them from Cleveland the year before I had begged them to take good care of themselves, saying, "I get so panicky about you sometimes." They had made a sacrifice to let me go away for the two years, wanting to broaden my horizon. It would give them great joy if I remained with them this year. I did not yet know what I wanted to do with my life, though I did have some thought of further graduate work.

In the end I decided that, for this one year, I would stay at home. I had done my best to make the right decision. Now, according to my "bargain," providence would have a chance to "work things out all right." I could not know that providence was not only working things out in the best possible way but was doing it on an excellent schedule. That fall was exactly the right time for me to meet my future husband.

I was quite happy that October falling back into the loved pattern of home life with my father and mother. With no studying to do, I lost all trace of being a "grind" and gave myself up to a gay, sociable existence, something which it was easy to do in a Southern college town. My diary records a succession of picnics, expeditions up mountains, attending football games, bridge parties, and dances. Two young men who had graduated from Roanoke College, Joel Borden and Ray Adams, were back as instructors, and they made up a gay foursome with my friend Frances Koiner and me. We spent many evenings together, going to entertainments or playing cards at home. Our lightheartedness is apparent in what we called this companionable foursome, the S.I.S. (Self Improvement Society) whose purpose, we said with mock solemnity, was the prevention of social error! There was also a larger group of young people, with another most willing escort, with whom I was going places and having fun.

For the first time since I had graduated, I was in town when Dr. Randall was. In the summers, when I had been at home, he had been away for research and vacation. In the meantime a tragedy had come into his life. His wife, a former classmate of his at Butler College named Edith Abbott, had died the fall I went to Indiana University. She had had much painful illness and two major operations before her marriage. In the second surgery her chances of recovery had seemed very slight, and after a third operation in October 1913, she died from shock. They had been married just two years. My mother wrote me about her death and I felt very sorry for him in an impersonal way, for he was still a stranger to me whom I knew only by sight. I had never spoken to him.

My mother and father had come to know him well, however. My mother had learned from his landlady how sad and lonely he was. He could not bear to go to parties or other social engagements and was leading a joyless existence, devoting himself only to his teaching and research. But some way he had discovered how many congenial interests he had with my father and how kind and sympathetic both of my parents were, and he liked to come for quiet visits with them. Writing to me later and speaking of those two "dreary years" when "I kept awfully to myself," he said, "It was a fine thing to be so welcome in the Painter home — even before I knew you." It had meant much to him, he continued, "to feel that there was an entree for me at 166 High Street."

So it happened on Sunday, October 24, 1915, when I returned home in the afternoon after having dinner with a group of friends, I found that my father and mother had a caller. When I entered the room my father said, "Dr. Randall, this is my daughter Ruth." Providence could not possibly have designed a more proper introduction than that! I knew from the college annual that this gentleman had gone to Butler College and that Dr. Howe, with whom I had done my graduate work at Indiana University, had previously taught there, so I said: "I think we have both studied under the same

Jim's Parents and Jim When Very Young

Above, Ellen Kregelo Randall and Horace Randall. Below,
Jim when about four, with his baby sister Mary.

delightful English professor, Dr. Howe." It developed
that we both admired Dr. Howe immensely and enjoyed
talking about him. But so blind was I to the workings of
providence that my diary for that day, while giving
every other detail, does not even mention meeting Dr.
Randall!

Two weeks later I was much surprised to have him
phone and ask me to take a walk with him out the
Hanging Rock road. His name appears in my diary for
the first time on the date of that walk, November 8. The
road was a beautiful wooded one and I still have the
watercolor sketch he made of it later for sentimental
reasons. It shows a curve in a road on a hillside, a road
tinged with the red clay of Virginia and bordered by
goldenrod. Above it and below are green pine trees and
in the distance a glimpse of blue mountain. Months later
when we were engaged I wrote him: "I love that road
even if a certain gentleman of whom I stood much in
awe (then) made me walk along it so fast, once upon a
time, that I didn't recover for a week!" He was a fast
walker and I a slow one but I did not like to mention it.
We were both a bit shy on that first date.

On November 14 he took me to an afternoon dramatic performance at Elizabeth College, a girls' college in
Salem. When we returned, my mother, with her usual
hospitality, invited him to stay for supper. He left early,
much to my relief, for I had a date with another gentleman that evening! The next day I left town for a short
visit with my sister Margaret at Marion, Virginia, and on
the day of my return I recorded in my diary: "Found a

beautiful bouquet of chrysanthemums here from Dr. Randall." Three days later he called, bringing a record for our Victrola. It was, as I remember, "Drink to Me Only with Thine Eyes."

My diaries from then on are sprinkled with his name. Few courtships have left such complete documentation as ours. The day-by-day diaries record the actual events, usually without comment. But better still, during our long engagement when we were not together, we were to write each other voluminous letters in which we lived over again the precious incidents which had brought about such a miracle in our lives. (When I was writing my biography of Mrs. Custer, *I Elizabeth*, I found she and General Custer, during their engagement, had done exactly the same thing.) Our letters tell our thoughts and feelings about those events at every stage of the courtship. They use a new language, the universal language of a couple who are deeply in love with each other; they employ certain expressions all their own. For instance, after I once quoted to him something I had read in a favorite book: "Love is not a Cupid; love is a Giant," the word "giant" appears frequently as a synonym for love.

What was happening to us that winter of 1915–1916 is made clear in two quotations from these letters. He realized very quickly that he had fallen in love. I was slow to reach that state and slow to recognize it when I did reach it. He wrote me in happy retrospect: "I wonder if you know what it means to me to be lifted out of that homeless feeling I did have. . . . I met *you* and very soon came to love you." I wrote him: "How unconscious I was of the trick the Giant was playing on me. One of the things I am gladdest of is that my friendship and admiration for you slipped so gradually into love that I did not realize it."

In January 1916, I was finding the situation a bit confusing. Two young men around my own age were having as many dates with me as Dr. Randall was, a fact that was causing him considerable anxiety. (It was needless worry, for I was not involved emotionally with either one.) I knew he was older than I was, though I did not then know the exact difference in our ages, eleven years and four months. He was a professor and there was a certain formality between us. He called me Miss Painter and I addressed him as Dr. Randall, while I called my other escorts by their first names. He had found something vital to live for after two years of mere existence and he almost had to learn over again to let go and be lighthearted. Of course, I knew how he felt about me, and I was carefully holding him off from telling me, as I did not yet know how I felt about him. I wrote him later in one of my retrospective letters: "You kept me interested from the first, Jim, but . . . I think I must have tried to resist my liking for you."

On January 21 there occurred an event which we later looked upon as a sort of milestone in the courtship. That night I wrote in my diary: "In evening went with Dr. Randall to Roanoke to hear Fritz Kreisler. Had an ideally happy evening." We had evidently dressed in our best for the occasion, as the diary continues: "Dr. R.

looked very nice in his dress suit, the music was wonderful beyond words and the companionship was good."

On the first anniversary of this date I wrote my fiancé, Jim, a much more effusive account of the occasion when we heard the famous violinist: "I have never been quite able to express the sweet uniqueness of that evening. Somehow we seemed perfectly in tune, and I remember, most distinctly of all, the feeling I had when we said goodnight at the front steps. It was a damp misty night and yet light, so that I could see you quite well, and as I held out my hand, a little compound feeling of reluctance to have you go, and a realization of how perfectly happy and congenial I had been with you swept over me, and I guess if that designing old giant of ours was peeping into my mind then he must have patted himself on the back."

This was, of course, written in the light of my subsequent feeling for him. Elsewhere in another letter, I sized up the situation at that time very accurately. I said I believed that evening was the first time the giant had touched me "and it was such a gentle little touch that I didn't recognize him for a giant at all."

I was not yet in love and I was afraid he was. I certainly did not want to hurt this gentle, lovable man. Perhaps it would be a good thing if I left town for a while. So, in the middle of February, I went to Harrisburg, Pennsylvania, to visit my sister Elizabeth and her minister husband, who was pastor of Messiah Lutheran Church there.

5.

Engagement Accomplished Under Difficulties

Few people could be better company than Elizabeth and Henry. I had a wonderful three weeks with them, going to luncheons, dinners, plays, and even a fire at which I got thoroughly soaked with water from a fireman's hose. The second week in March had begun by the time I returned to Salem. I had had two letters from Dr. Randall while I was away, and I was greeted with a florist's box of red carnations from him on my return.

Springtime in Virginia is always lovely, but that seems to me now the climactic spring of my girlhood. I no longer worried over the situation but fell back on my old resolution to let providence work things out. I saw a great deal of Dr. Randall, who, with great wisdom, did not talk of love. He merely went on quietly calling at my home or taking me places several times a week and making himself indispensable to me in a hundred different ways. He told me later that he "was delighted with the sweet way our friendship was developing" and felt it was best to let things go on as they were for a while. I was unconsciously getting fonder and fonder of him.

We had such good times together! We walked out to the spring woods to hunt for the fragrant pink arbutus which is found under the winter's dead leaves and usually on the north side of a hill. It was a sort of treasure hunt. We went on drives up Twelve O'Clock Knob with a horse and buggy, the only vehicle which could travel those mountain roads at that time. It was a drive of inexpressible beauty. The mountain wall of untouched forest rose steeply above us on one side of the narrow road, and fell off like a precipice on the other. At some places we could look down on the fair valley far below; at others on range upon range of blue mountains. The mountain air had a quality all its own which was like a tonic.

Jim's natural cheerful personality had now emerged fully from the shadow. Two years of devoting himself to his work without play had understandably left him somewhat overserious. I must have tried to bring him out of this, for later he wrote me describing what he called my "revolt from high-brow-ism." He said that when he began to be "professorish" and talk "about encyclopedias and such," I would clasp my hands resignedly and say, "Yes, Professor." He continued: "There's something very delightful about your interest in things 'frivolous'; that is to say, in things *human*."

Gradually, when I went on group outings with my friends, Dr. Randall was included. Once three couples of us had a picnic on the very top of Twelve O'Clock Knob, cooking our supper over a fire and going home by moonlight. Once four of us drove over to Hollins College, about nine miles from Salem, to attend a picturesque Shakespeare pageant. He learned to play bridge because I liked it, and we occasionally had an evening game with friends.

We both loved books and sometimes read together in the evenings. He was ambitious to do historical writing, and I was tremendously interested in the articles he planned to write and the book which would be an outgrowth of his doctoral thesis. I loved to talk to him about these things. I was making new discoveries about him all the time. He had a keen sense of humor and could be very witty and droll. We saw the same funny side of things and laughed together. We had fun teasing each other or indulging in whimsical make-believe.

The gossips of the town and college were having a field day watching this professorial wooing, especially as my occasional dates with other escorts suggested a rivalry. It seemed to be an approving interest, however, for we both had many friends, and their consensus was that we were perfectly suited to each other. I suspect that they were guessing at the wedding date before we were even engaged.

The happy days drifted into the month of June. By that time I was calling Dr. Randall "Jim." The summer gathering of the clan commenced with the arrival of two sisters for a visit — Margaret and Laura with her lively little son, Dick. Jim was always invited for dinner or

supper if he was around, which he usually was, and very
quickly he became acquainted with them at the dining
table. I recorded in my diary how much they liked him.

It was his usual custom to leave Salem in June to visit
his mother and the rest of his family in Indianapolis. It
was probably the realization of how much I would miss
him when he left that woke me up to the knowledge that
I loved him. I do not see now how I could have been so
blind as I was up to that time. How blank the days
would be when he was gone! What would I do without
his gentle and understanding companionship? I had
finally reached the point where I was ready to listen to
his proposal and become engaged to him. Jim later told
me that he had made up his mind to get an answer from
me before he left Salem that summer. So it looked as if
the stage was all set. At this juncture our special providence seemingly developed a sense of humor and introduced an amusing complication!

A couple of years previously Jim had told his little
nephew, Ralph Randall, that if he would make the trip
from Indianapolis to Salem, he, Uncle Jim, would take
him to Natural Bridge and Mountain Lake and the two
of them would have a great old time together. Then
Uncle Jim would take the boy back home when he went
to Indianapolis for his usual family visit. Jim had not
intended to leave Salem as soon as usual this year, but his
family (who knew nothing of his courtship of me) was
not aware of that fact.

Suddenly Jim received a letter from his brother
Arthur, Ralph's father, saying that Ralph was coming.

Almost before he knew it, Jim had a twelve-year-old boy on his hands and promises to keep. He and I could not get a moment alone together! Our twosome had become a threesome. I was a complete surprise to Ralph, who had expected to have his Uncle Jim all to himself.

I shall never forget the comical buggy ride up Twelve O'Clock Knob which the three of us took on June 20. The buggy, like our courtship, was designed for two, not three. Ralph decided he would get out and perch himself up behind, thereby putting both of us on pins and needles for fear he would fall off and be hurt. I think the boy realized something of the situation and wanted to leave the two of us alone. The next development was a terrific downpour of rain. We hastily bundled Ralph inside the buggy, where all three of us sat crowded together, getting thoroughly soaked. My diary, with a nice choice of words, describes that drive as "interesting."

Jim next took Ralph on the promised visit to Natural Bridge for a couple of days. The following Saturday, June 24, was Jim's birthday, and he and his nephew had been invited to have dinner at the Painter home on that date. I baked a big birthday cake the afternoon before and was busy trying to make it a very special dinner. It would have to be served promptly at one o'clock, as the two of them were to catch a train to Pembroke, Virginia, at three-thirty. Pembroke was the little station where one got off to be taken up the mountainside in a horse-drawn vehicle to Mountain Lake. Since Pembroke was on the way west, it was logical for them, after their visit to the resort, to go on from there to Indianapolis.

It was a very lively group which gathered around our dining table that twenty-fourth of June. Margaret and Laura were a whole gay team in themselves, and also very understanding and cooperative. They proved this after dinner by tactfully whisking Ralph off to the front porch, while Jim and I vanished into my father's study. Our face-saving pretext was that Jim must not let Ralph see him smoking as that would set the boy a bad example.

I don't think either of us had noticed that outdoors there was a gathering storm. Providence apparently was set on making this part of our courtship a comedy of circumstances. Some time previously Jim had brought me a record of an old love song, "Last Night," with the vague idea (as he told me later) of using it as background music on the occasion when, or if, I would promise to be his wife. Instead, we were to have, as background effects for our tender scene, thunder and lightning!

We had scarcely seated ourselves and begun to talk when there was the interruption of a telephone call. That had to be attended to, and again we sat down in the study. Jim began to speak with deep emotion. (The next day he wrote me from Mountain Lake: "I had *so much to say* during those precious moments when I could linger in Salem and I now realize how inadequate was my attempt to say it. But I'll declare, dear, there *was* something romantic in the whole situation — the shortness of the time, the retreat into the study, the interruptions, the excitement of the thunderstorm, the telephoning, etc., etc.")

I was feeling very emotional myself at that scene in the study, and when I answered him, it was "in a wee small voice." Later I would not let him describe what he had said as "inadequate." I wrote back: "I know every word you said, my sweetheart, and not for anything would I have a single word of that different. I doubt if you know how beautiful your way of telling me was."

We had scarcely finished opening our hearts to each other when the storm broke in full force. The sky was split apart by jagged streaks of lightning and the thunder was terrific. The weather gave the new engagement a regular Fourth of July celebration!

The time arrived for the travelers to start to the station. Ralph was greatly relieved to see his Uncle Jim reappear. He had been well entertained by my two resourceful sisters but had kept asking, "Where's Uncle Jim?" without getting a satisfactory answer. There was the flurry of getting the two off in a taxi and my diary frankly records that the rest of that day "I hardly know what I did!"

The way we both felt next day can be best described by two quotations from *The Mikado:* "Here's a how-de-do!" "Here's a state of things!" Minutes after we had become engaged, we had been parted with a thousand and one tender confessions we wanted to make to each other unsaid. This could not be endured. Jim wrote his brother Arthur that an important matter had come up

Four Pictures Taken During Our Engagement

The cat in the picture below, right, was my Maltese, Don.
I would say, "Kiss me, Don," and he would lift his head to
rub it against my cheek.

which required his return to Salem. He would therefore put Ralph on the train at Pembroke and would Arthur please meet him at the point where he had to change trains in Ohio. Two dozen lovely roses came to me on Monday, and a week later Jim himself reappeared. In the following days I wrote in my diary that the word "happy" did not begin to express our feelings. "The more we talk things over, serious and light things," I wrote, "the more perfect our union seems to be."

There was one serious matter on which we had to make a decision at once. Some time previously Jim had applied for the Harrison Research Fellowship at the University of Pennsylvania and now, with the same inopportuneness as Ralph's visit, he received that appointment. If he accepted it, he would have to be in Philadelphia the academic year of 1916–1917. When should we be married?

Jim asked me whether I would go with him to Philadelphia and gave me all the facts about his finances. He had earned his own way through his graduate work at the University of Chicago, and on the small salary he received at Roanoke College he had been able to save but little. The year in Philadelphia would give him a chance to work on articles and his first book, and we agreed then, as we always would later, that his work must come first, even if it did mean sacrifices. It was definitely his ambition to teach and write in a large university and it was only by publishing scholarly work that he would be able to do this. We decided that our marriage would have to be postponed until the following year.

After he left Salem for the rest of the summer, each daily record in my diary included "Wrote to Jim." Reading these letters written just after we became engaged, I am struck by the fact that we both had a feeling we were not worthy of the miraculous thing which had happened to us. I had led such a sheltered life that I was undoubtedly immature in many ways, and now, facing "the responsibility of being a Mrs.," I began to realize this. In one letter in which I asked if he would teach me to swim, I continued: "I'm afraid you will have to teach me a great many other things too. Sometimes I am overwhelmed with the fear of being inadequate, of failing you in many respects, and it makes me wish I were more grown-up than I feel."

His tender letter which came with the engagement ring includes the same thought on his part. He wrote: "With the ring there goes a world of love, and a prayer, too. . . . I am the proudest man on earth to feel that you will be wearing this ring. . . . there's nothing engraved on it (you can just remember who gave it to you)." The letter ends: "I'm not worthy of the privilege of giving you this ring, Ruth, but in one respect I *can* qualify — *I love you* with all the loving adverbs that the language contains, — and more!"

Laura left Salem about the middle of August to return to her home in Platteville, Wisconsin, and I went with her for a long visit. By this time a most welcome plan had been worked out. Jim would come to Platteville in September before going to Philadelphia. He arrived on

September 12 and my diary for the ten glorious days
which followed fairly overflows with happiness.

Laura and Harold, the best of companions, planned
one delightful expedition after another. Harold's work
took him to all the lead mines for miles around and we
loved to go adventuring with him. Once Jim and I,
donning old coats, rubber boots, and caps with miners'
lights, went with Harold down the dark hole of a shaft
to the depth of a hundred and twenty feet, where we
were shown the whole process of lead mining. My diary
described the scene: "There was something very impressive about those big black-walled underground
chambers with their thick darkness thru which the tiny
miners' lights flitted weirdly and ineffectively." We explored neighboring towns, went on picnics, and on fishing expeditions, for we all loved to fish. Best of all each
"wonderful day was ended by a wonderful evening in
which we plan for our little home and the time when we
shall be partners."

Like all engaged couples we sat on a sofa together —
"playing sofa," we called it — and one evening something happened which we found hilariously funny. It
concerned Laura's fox terrier, Pepper, who was very
affectionate and extremely jealous. Pepper had never
quite forgiven Laura for having that baby, Dick, and
when I, who loved dogs, appeared, Pepper adopted me.
Then Jim came to town and Pepper regarded him as a
rival for my affections. So one evening as we sat on the
sofa Pepper jumped on my lap and began to squirm.
Suddenly we realized what the dog was doing; he was

squeezing between us and trying to push Jim off the sofa! Jim refused to be ejected and leaned over Pepper to kiss me, at which Pepper gave a loud groan. Shaking with silent laughter, Jim repeated the performance and each time our canine chaperone would let out one of those awful groans. We had lots of fun that evening!

The time passed all too quickly until he left Platteville for Philadelphia and I returned to Salem. Our communication was then reduced to writing. Personal letters are often self-portraits and it seems to me now we each unconsciously sketched our own personalities in the letters we exchanged in the months which followed. At least, through these letters, we learned to know each other much more fully than before.

From the first we had each seemed anxious for the other to know his or her failings. A month after we became engaged he had written me warning me he sometimes had "peeved spells." He promptly received a spirited answer: "As to the time when I shall encounter one of your 'peeved' spells, Prof. Jim, this is all I have to say: I have some ability in that line myself! Suppose we make a bargain never to get peeved at the same time. Then I will always take care to beat you to it!" I feel sure he chuckled over this, as nothing delighted him more than to "get a rise" from me. About the same time I broke the news to him that I too sometimes got out of sorts. I began one letter like this: "I feel this morning exactly like the little boy who slipped into the empty church, sat down in the Amen corner and said, 'Darn it!' "

It disturbed me when he continued to undervalue himself in passages like this: "I hesitate to ask myself what there is about me that you could love. . . ." He seemed to me completely without vanity. In the years ahead I would sometimes tell him that I wished I could inoculate him with a little germ of self-esteem, adding quickly that I would be extremely careful not to give an overdose!

Jim was thin and his shoulders had a scholar's droop when I first met him. After we became engaged and a new life full of vital interest opened up before him, he began a systematic effort to build himself up. His letters from Philadelphia tell of his going to the gym regularly for exercise. My letters to him speak constantly of my sending him cakes, cookies, nut bread and other tempting things in the hope of increasing his weight.

He had been a heavy smoker and I was anxious for him to cut down on his smoking. Evidently I frequently reminded him of this and, as he put it, of other "things that need straightening out." He called it "scolding" and added that his fiancée looked especially pretty "when she gets her scolding togs on." He was doing his best to improve, he wrote, and would endure the scolding provided he could claim his "reward for such submissive acquiescence."

As was natural in a person so sensitive, Jim suffered at times, when under strain, from nervous tension. He admitted this and added that for a long time he had been without any one who "particularly cared whether my work caused me strain or not." It meant so much to him, he wrote, that now there was one who cared. It was only a sweetheart or wife, he said, who could enter into one's life fully and "take an interest in all the little things that make up life."

An increasing amount of space in these letters is devoted to what we finally called our "literary companionship." He was writing a number of articles that year and would send them to me for suggestions. Enclosing an early one he wrote: "There's a feeling that I can't quite express that causes me to want to show this to you as soon as I have finished it." After reading two of his articles which he sent together that fall, I wrote: "I am slowly getting acquainted with this gentleman to whom I am engaged. . . . The style of both [articles] was very, very fine, a style of real literary gift I think." Reading a letter of mine shortly after he went to Philadelphia, he believed he had made a similar discovery: "The thought came to me today — what a fine style my sweetheart has, considered from the literary standpoint." Dealing progressively with this favorite topic of literary companionship, we both became unconsciously prophetic of the future. "We *can* work together in things literary," he wrote, continuing with the statement that he wanted someday to depend upon me for "the real literary touch" and he was sure there would be "some literary job" in the future with which he could help me.

A letter which I wrote in the spring before we were married went deeply into the subject. I began by telling him that I had been working over "a little literary composition" with my father. "I want to tell you," I said, "of the joy it brings for two people to work together over something creative, to test each word, to suggest different ways of expression, and to feel working within them that instinct by which they know whether a thing is true literary expression or not. I can't quite express that joy, but you know yourself what I mean." I continued with considerable emotion: "Dear, my eyes are wet when I think of you and myself working together in that way over some article you have written. . . . I want to keep myself fit to be a help to you. . . . Just to talk of this way of being partners gives me one of the realest thrills of happiness that any anticipation of the future can."

Apropos of his writing articles while I was making things for my hope chest, this passage appears in one of my letters in the fall of 1916: "Let's play we are living in a fairy tale and our Giant has assigned us these tasks to accomplish before our wedding day. We will have to be diligent and work with a will, as the story books say, but each day brings us nearer the time when we shall 'live happy ever after.' "

We dreamed constantly of each other and wrote about our dreams. Amusingly Jim objected to one dream I had: "You did peeve me a little by that dream in which you got angry with your husband." But he continued forgivingly: "I'd better say that I'll not begrudge you the pleasure which I suppose every wife wants to claim, of quarrelling with her inferior half!"

There can be little doubt that these letters are very revealing. Above all they are love letters, as letters between two people who are planning to be married should be. They show that my devotion to him was deepening and that I knew this. "I have come to realize," I wrote him, "how love grows by loving." Late in November he read these words from me: "My heart will be full of a true Thanksgiving tomorrow for this: I have found my partner in life, and found him strong and noble and tender; so that I trust him completely and am proud of him. . . ."

He came to Salem for an all-too-brief visit at Christmas and left on December 26 to attend a meeting of the American Historical Association. So we were apart when the New Year of 1917 came in, the year in which we were to be married. On New Year's Eve, looking back, he wrote: "The grandest things in life — love and happiness — are what this dear old year has offered." He looked forward to the coming year, he said, with a "veritable glory of anticipation" and also with a prayer that he would be worthy "of the beautiful wife who is to put her hand in mine and say the sweet words so full of significance."

Yet early in that year we just missed having a serious lovers' quarrel!

6.

An Almost Quarrel, a Wedding, and a Honeymoon

The trouble arose from what we called "getting down to brass tacks." In other words, we were trying to work out a budget which would enable us to keep house on Jim's salary of fifteen hundred dollars a year. That figure seems ridiculous now but it did not then when a dollar bought so much more than today. Faculty families all around us were living on it, though they had to practice economy.

In working on the budget Jim wrote his sister Alice, who with her husband, Walter E. Jenney, was making a very happy home on limited means. He asked her how her budget ran. She answered him fully and cheerfully and her letter included this sentence: "If there were no hard problems to be solved, we would all be weaklings. . . ."

I was also collecting information on budgets. I had a good friend who had married a professor the year before and whose circumstances were parallel to what mine would be. So about this time I asked her how her housekeeping expenses worked out. She advised me in the strongest terms not to try it but to board. Keeping house in Salem in a house that had few or no conveniences was laborious, she told me; servants were hard to get, and wages and prices were going up.

In the misunderstanding which followed Jim and I each made a blunder. My blunder was to write him all that my friend had said. I should have realized that he was sensitive about the fact that he had so little to offer me financially and that he might interpret my letter as a hint to postpone our marriage. I ought to have known better!

He did so misinterpret my letter and was dreadfully hurt. His blunder was to answer it immediately before he had time to reflect. His answer used some plain language about working out our problems ourselves and not letting other people's opinions influence me. He offered to postpone our marriage, if that was what I wanted. Such a thought had not occurred to me; I was taking the budget-making as a sort of interesting game. Worst of all, he quoted from his sister's letter, using that word "weakling." He should have known better than that!

I in my turn was terribly hurt. I began my answer to him by saying I felt exactly as if I had been spanked. "Your let-lecture came half an hour ago," I continued, "and I will confess that its first reading brought a tear or two that dried up in a flash of temper. But on the second reading I knew you were only saying to me to brace up and be a woman." I admitted I was at fault in allowing pessimistic views of other people to color my own. "So I took my medicine, Jim, even if it did hurt."

I assured him that if he could see me working on my towels and pillowcases he would know how far I was from any thought of postponing our marriage or giving up the idea of our having a little home of our own. His suggestion about waiting, I said, "hurt the deepest. I feel in that hurt the reflection of the hurt which I have given you in some of my pessimistic remarks about our problem. I am so sorry about that, dear, so sorry."

I had something to say about his use of that word "weakling." I told him my life had been too sheltered "to have any tests larger than those of college or university problems, but I don't believe I have ever been considered either a weakling or a quitter." Further on I returned to the subject in lighter tone. If the conditions were ever reversed, I said, and he ever provoked me as much as I had provoked him by my letter which started all this, I would give him "such a rousing lecture in return that you won't have further fears about a weakling!" I signed myself "Your chastened but devoted Ruth."

Knowing him so well, I suspected that he would hate himself as soon as he had mailed his scolding letter to me. It had arrived on a Saturday and unless I sent my reply special delivery he would spend a miserable Sunday reproaching himself. So I walked downtown that afternoon to mail my answer. It crossed his special delivery filled with remorse and begging me to forgive him for the reproving letter which he had sent to me!

He answered my special delivery at once and in a mood of "intensified love" in response to its "gentleness." He also liked the "spirit" of it: "The scene would have been imperfect without that 'flash of temper.'" He was not telling me to "brace up and be a woman," he went on. He had never even "dreamed of associating the word weakling" with me. What had really angered him was the pessimistic advice my friend had given me. "Why in all conscience hasn't *some* one presented to you those elements of the housekeeping and brass-tack proposition that are encouraging!" His "too emphatic letter" was a matter of "painful regret" to him. He was so sorry about the whole thing; would I please try to forget about it? This is a very loving letter and so is the one in which I wrote a paragraph that makes a pleasant conclusion to this account of an almost lovers' quarrel: "Dear, don't you see that the first occasion between us where there might have been anger and real misunderstanding was averted because each of us at once was filled with a tender thought to prevent the other's hurt. It's a nice little prophecy of what our future 'quarrels' will be like, isn't it?"

The letters quoted above were written in the second week of February 1917, when we had both come under the strain of a great new anxiety. Early in February the United States had broken diplomatic relations with Germany. In my letter of the ninth I wrote how "one big ominous topic" overshadowed all others, "the prospect of war." It made me heartsick to read the papers, I continued. "When I remember . . . what individuals in war suffer and will have to suffer, it seems too terrible even to think about." On April 6 the United States declared war with Germany. The First World War was upon us.

This changed the orientation of all our thoughts for the future. War is like a great conflagration in which the cherished life plans of individuals beyond number are consumed like so many matchsticks. In May Jim wrote about the draft bill leaving him out. In other words, he was above the age limit. Two weeks later he said: "I wish the way were open for some kind of national service I could enter. . . . I have 'filled out blanks' and applied for various things." From that time on he was helping the war effort in every way he could, and ultimately he got a full-time position in war work. The war eventually uprooted us and temporarily changed the course of our lives.

Rising prices began to affect our budget-making. In January 1917, before the rise, I had enclosed in a letter to Jim the estimated budget which my parents and I had worked out together. The figures seem impossible now. We allowed twenty dollars a month for rent and fifty for food. For clothes for us both the annual amount was two hundred and ninety dollars. Domestic help, light, heat, and water were all listed and the amount left out of his salary for recreation and sundries was forty-five dollars! In the letter which went with this estimate I remarked that "brass tacks often have sharp points."

Nevertheless we continued to plan for a little house of our own. Where it would be located, we did not know, as there were no apartments in Salem and almost no houses for rent. At one point I suggested to Jim that he find out what rent Peter paid for the pumpkin shell with which he settled his similar problem! As spring went into summer, our letters were crowded with matters that had to be worked out under the uncertainty and distress of the war.

There were complications even about setting the date for the wedding. We had thought vaguely of getting married in June but again providence interposed a delay. Jim received an offer to teach at Syracuse University that summer and we needed the extra money which that would bring. So we had to choose a date after the summer session was over. Afterwards I used to say jokingly that we had to get married at a time when it did not interfere with anything important! On August 2 the *Roanoke Times* reported that invitations were out for the marriage of Ruth Elaine Painter, "daughter of one of Virginia's most distinguished men of letters," to Mr. James Garfield Randall on Tuesday, August 21, at 9 o'clock in the evening, at College Church, Salem, Virginia.

The remaining days until that date were very exciting. The house began to fill up. The first to arrive were Julia and Arch by car, bringing one of my bridesmaids, Louise Edgar. My other three sisters could not be present at the ceremony, being involved, or about to be involved, with young babies. Boy, however, would come to be in the wedding party and Jim's mother would make the trip from Indianapolis to attend.

Presents were arriving constantly. My wedding dress, made in Louisville, Kentucky, was delivered and produced a regular chorus of ohs and ahs. My girlhood friends, two of whom had given showers for me, kept running in to see my trousseau and the presents.

My hurried diary entry for August 19 shows the tempo of events: "Jim arrived at ten. We went to the station with Mama & Arch a little after eleven. Boy got off of one train at 11:28, and Jim's mother off of another at 11:43. All were here for dinner." I loved Jim's gentle, responsive little mother at once and she seemed more than ready to love me. Perhaps it was for a special reason. She had been deeply worried over Jim's period of loneliness and I think she blessed me in her heart for bringing happiness into his life again.

When we reached home, of course there were introductions all around. Boy and Louise both loved to tease, and when they met they at once entered into a conspiracy to give the bride and groom a hilarious send-off at the railroad station. There were conspiratorial whispers and ominous hints such as "Did you get plenty of rice?" were thrown out for Jim's and my benefit.

On the evening of August 20 we had a rehearsal at the church, followed by an elaborate party at Frances Koiner's home. The church stood at the very center of the little town, across from Dillard's drugstore in front and across from the courthouse on the side. The next day friends decorated it beautifully with white flowers and tall white cathedral candles.

My father was to perform the ceremony, as he had for my four sisters. He was qualified to do this because, as a young man, he had first planned to be a minister and had graduated from a theological seminary before he decided to be a professor instead. The wedding party included two members of that playful organization the S.I.S., Frances Koiner and Ray Adams. Julia would be dame of honor, Jim's colleague Professor A. P. Wagener, best man, and I would enter on the arm of my brother-in-law Arch Throckmorton.

I remember well the emotion I felt as I stood at the door holding Arch's arm and waiting to start down the long church aisle which had known the bridal footsteps of my four sisters. At this moment there came a dramatic effect which had not been planned. The deep-toned clock in the tower of the courthouse across the street slowly and solemnly pealed the hour of nine. At the last stroke the first strains of the *Lohengrin* wedding march began and the wedding party entered.

There lies before me now a long clipping from the *Salem Times-Register and Sentinel,* the town's once-a-week newspaper. It is a detailed, friendly, even flattering, account of our wedding. The bride is described as "one of the most charming and most cultured of the young ladies of Salem," the groom as "a valued member of the faculty of Roanoke College." It tells how the ladies were dressed: "Mrs. A. H. Throckmorton, a sister

The Way We Looked

These pictures, though taken before our engagement, give
a good idea of how Jim and I looked at the time of our
wedding.

of the bride, as dame of honor, wore a lovely costume of blue Georgette crepe and tulle with beaded bodice. She carried a shower bouquet of Killarney roses tied with pink ribbon." The account continues about the bride: "She was more than lovely in her wedding gown of white duchess satin en traine and trimmed with silver lace. Her tulle veil was caught about her head with orange blossoms and she carried a beautiful shower bouquet of bride roses, gardenias and jasmine. She was met at the altar by Dr. Randall. . . ."

We stood together before my father. I heard his loved voice repeat the ever-solemn words of the marriage service: "I Ruth take thee James . . . for better for worse, for richer for poorer, in sickness and in health, to love and to cherish, till death us do part." Perhaps my lips trembled a little as I made my responses and my hand on Jim's arm could feel the tenseness of his emotion. When the wedding ring engraved "Jim to Ruth" had been slipped on my finger and the last "sweet words so full of significance" were ended, the music boomed out triumphantly and suddenly all was gaiety and excitement again. As the clipping says: "The ceremony was followed by a reception at the hospitable home of Dr. and Mrs. Painter." There was a hilarious cutting of the huge wedding cake. Tiny silver objects had been baked in it: a thimble which signified an old maid, a button for a bachelor, and a little silver heart which meant a happy marriage. Jim and I had all the ancient good-luck signs with us on our wedding day, bright sunshine, a cricket chirping on the hearth in the parlor that evening, and I myself got the little silver heart in my piece of cake. I still have it.

When the time came for Jim and me to go upstairs to change our clothes, the archconspirators, Boy and Louise, and two or three other merrymakers, became very watchful. They knew nothing of our plans but they figured the only train we could take was one leaving Roanoke at midnight. This meant we would have to be driven to Roanoke and they had their car in readiness to follow us. Julia and Arch were on our side to help outwit them and their car also was in readiness. Fortunately there were two roads from Salem to Roanoke. If we could only get a head start and lose them, they would not know which road we had taken.

Somehow we managed to get out the door and into the Throckmorton car before the mischief-makers were quite aware of what was happening. We drove fast for the first mile or two and still did not see the lights of any other car following us. They had to guess now which road we had taken and they guessed wrong.

There was something else they did not know; we were not going to take any train that night but planned to stay in Roanoke and take a train the next morning. Julia and Arch took us to the Hotel Roanoke, where, for the first time I saw Jim register Mr. and Mrs. J. G. Randall. The merrymakers went to the railroad station, boarded the midnight train when it came in, woke up the passengers in the Pullman, and peeped into the drawing room to the great indignation of the elderly couple who occupied it. They found no trace of bride and groom. We chuckled to think how we had outwitted them.

We took the Memphis Special the next morning on our way south. Jim had selected for our honeymoon Lake Junaluska in North Carolina. He loved swimming and boating and for him a vacation was not a vacation unless it included both. He could not have chosen a more beautiful spot. "The lake," I wrote in my diary, "is set in wooded hills with mountains rising on every side."

We stayed at the Junaluska Inn, which was on a hill overlooking the lake. There, for two golden weeks, we put war and brass tacks out of our minds and gave ourselves up to living in the completely satisfying present. We took exploring hikes, and went on expeditions to neighboring places. We spent long hours in our boat on the lake. Jim took a daily swim and gave me swimming lessons which were lots of fun but unsuccessful. On the last day of August I wrote in my diary: "There never were two people happier."

One thing, however, was hardly appropriate on a honeymoon. My bridegroom developed a boil on his chin! This explains why he is not in any of the pictures we took; they are all of me alone. We did, however, put his hat in one picture to show he was around! To take care of the boil he took a train to Waynesville to see a doctor, who lanced the painful thing and gave him some pills to take so many hours apart. And thereby hangs a tale with which Jim loved to tease me afterwards.

Seven days after we were married we took an evening row on the lake under a glorious full moon. No setting could have been more perfect. As we climbed the hill toward the hotel on our return, Jim pulled out his watch, which could easily be read in the bright moonlight. "Look," he said tenderly as he held it out to me, "it's nine o'clock." "That's right," I answered matter-of-factly. "It's pill time." "Pill time!" he exclaimed, indignant at my unromantic reply. "I meant we were married just one week ago at this very hour."

On September 3 I wrote in my diary: "It has been a perfect honeymoon, and we are very reluctant to leave Junaluska tomorrow. Jim has gained about four pounds and I have advanced from 102 pounds to 108!" We had both been thin at the time of the wedding. Now our holiday was over and we must get down again to everyday living and to "brass tacks."

I like to tell what my generous family had done to cushion the sharp points of those brass tacks. My father had solved our house problem. He owned a small dwelling at 96 High Street, less than two blocks away from our family home. It turned out that he could make it available to us at twenty dollars a month. He and my mother gave us as a wedding present complete mahogany furniture for dining room and bedroom. I was told to select exactly what I wanted. My sisters and brother gave us various pieces for the living room and Laura a silver tea set.

Until the house was ready for us, we were to stay at the old home where the whole upstairs was at our disposal. We fitted up one of the bedrooms as a study for Jim. He resumed his teaching at Roanoke College and, except for the heavy shadow of the war, everything for the newlyweds seemed ideal.

And then fate delivered a blow to us which very nearly proved fatal for me.

7.

Three Moves, "The Greatest Day Yet," and a Roast Goose for Christmas

Early in October Jim, who was writing an article for the *American Historical Review*, had to go to Washington for a few days to do some research for it. Several letters show that we took this first separation after our marriage rather hard. In one written just before his return he said, "My, but Wednesday will bring a sweet reunion!" The words were to prove cruelly ironic.

I was taken ill on Tuesday with a sore throat and high fever. It was late afternoon when the doctor came and took a culture. I had diphtheria again. Since the doctor had to drive to Roanoke to get the antitoxin, it was eleven o'clock at night before he returned to give it to me. There was no hospital in Salem, so I would have to be quarantined at home with a big sign on the front door, and my valiant little mother would again nurse me through it. Knowing Jim would arrive very early Wednesday, I asked the doctor not to put the sign up until after he returned.

The antitoxin threw me into what is called anaphylactic shock and I was desperately ill that night. When Jim, with eager face, hurried up the front walk early the next morning, my mother met him at the door with the news that I was ill. He could not even come into the room where I was. I remember how he stood in the doorway with anguished face and, scarcely knowing what he was saying, begged me to promise him I would get well. My condition was so critical that the doctor came three times that day. Perhaps the fact that I had so much happiness to live for was what tipped the scales in my favor.

I weathered the crisis and gradually improved. It was a wonderful day when the quarantine was lifted and Jim came into the room and carried me upstairs where he could take care of me. For days I lay on a couch close beside his desk in his temporary study while he worked on his article, occasionally stopping to put out his hand to touch me.

My illness prevented our moving into the house at 96 High Street (which we now called the Annex) until November. Jim was boyishly happy as we set up our housekeeping. Every trivial detail brought him pleasure. When our first bottle of milk was delivered he brought it in with beaming face, held it up, and said, "Look what somebody left on our porch!" When we acquired any additional article for the home, such as a new lamp or chair, according to my diary, "we had a jubilee" over it.

Housekeeping was light, as we were always more than welcome to have dinner with my father and mother or we could go to the college commons for meals. I was busy with war work, making surgical supplies at the Red Cross headquarters and knitting khaki-colored sweaters for the soldiers at home. Jim was doing articles for the Committee on Public Information at Washington along with his teaching.

I shall never forget our first Christmas when we walked out to the woods and cut down our own Christmas tree. There was a light snow on the ground and this, with the forest which we had named "Our Little Pines," created a real Christmas atmosphere. Jim swung his ax with a flourish, cutting down two trees and then, talking, laughing, and sometimes running a few steps for sheer joy, we dragged them home over the snow. The second tree was, of course, for my father and mother.

We really celebrated Christmas that year, decorating the trees at both houses. We lighted the little wax candles on our tree the evening of December 23 and those at the family home on Christmas Eve, for my parents and Jim and I were all starting to Philadelphia on Christmas Day. For us there was a double purpose in making this trip: We would attend the meeting of the American Historical Association, and also my brother's wedding to Anna Thomas on December 29. My diary records: "I loved Ann the minute I saw her."

Back in our own home in January we felt we had really become established married folks. I find in my diary that I used a new name for Jim now, "hubby" or "hubs," and he liked to call me his "commanding officer." We were shortly to find out, as married couples always do, that housekeeping involves many unexpected problems and crises. That was the coldest winter I had ever known in Salem and the Annex was an old house not built for below-zero weather. My diary entry for January 21, 1918, begins: "A day of trials and tribulations." We had gone out during the morning and when we returned to our porch, we heard water running inside the house. A frozen pipe had burst. To make matters worse, Jim had forgotten the key and we could not unlock the door, so he had to climb in a window. The diary continues: "Had a terrible time getting a plumber and before the water could be shut off, the cellar floor was covered and of course the bathroom was deluged. Took refuge up home getting dinner and supper and spending the night."

In less than a month Jim forgot the front door key again. I was beginning to suspect I had married an absentminded professor. This time the newlyweds put on quite a comedy act for the neighbors. Finding all windows on the first floor securely locked, Jim had to go up to my old home, borrow a ladder, and climb up to our second story. As he crawled through his study window, the two bird dogs next door raced madly up and down the fence proclaiming to high heaven that burglary was being committed right in front of their noses!

On February 21 I wrote in my diary: "We have been married six months today—the happiest six months of my life." Two events that spring encouraged us to feel that Jim was becoming better known as a historian. In March a telegram came asking if he would teach in the coming summer session at the University of Illinois. As he read it aloud to me I said, "Where is the University of Illinois?" and for the first time I heard the name Urbana, the town which was to become my future home. Of course we "had a jubilee" over that prospect. We hurried up to my parents' home to talk over the news but my father was out. I remember how we watched for him and ran to meet him halfway down the block, as I had so often done as a child. With one of us on each side of him we walked along telling him delightedly of this summer plan, and as always he joined in our enthusiasm.

The second heartening event "cast its shadow before" in my diary. Jim had been writing another article and on March 6 I wrote: "Helped Jim go over his article in morning, polishing it up. I read the rough draft aloud and we talk it over and make changes together." In the evening I dictated the article while he typed it and we mailed it off with high hopes the next day. Because of the war with Germany, it was a timely piece and we ardently wished that the *North American Review*, a prominent magazine at that time, would publish it. Its subject was "Germany's Censorship and News Control."

The magazine's acceptance came on April 26. Jim was

at the college when the mail arrived and I promptly took it over to him so that he would know the good news as soon as possible. I remember how proud I was that summer at the University of Illinois when the article appeared in print and a colleague said to Jim: "I take off my hat to anyone who can get an article in the *North American Review*."

Interspersed among the pleasant items in the diary, however, are frequent entries showing how war anxiety overshadowed everything. Three days after our elation over the article's acceptance I wrote: "These are fearfully anxious days on account of the great battle on the Western Front." Later I find: "The war rests on me like a pall." In wartime all joyousness seems muted, or, as I expressed it in my diary, we "would be quite happy if it were not for war fears."

That spring, working enthusiastically together with seeds and hoes, we planted flowers and vegetables in our garden, not knowing our sojourn in our first home would soon be ended. Because of the disruptions caused by the war, we were to live in three different cities in the space of three years.

Early in June we started west for Jim's summer teaching at the University of Illinois. Indianapolis was on our way to Urbana and we were to stop over and visit with Jim's people there. Meeting one's in-laws could be an ordeal but in my case it turned out to be a most happy experience, and I promptly wrote in my diary, "I love my new family." We arrived in time for Sunday dinner at the old Randall home at 2025 North Pennsylvania

Street and found the table set for twelve! Jim's mother (his father had died some time before), his two sisters, Alice and Mary, with their respective husbands, Walter Jenney and Homer Enlow, his brother Arthur with his wife Anna and their three children, Ralph, Ruth Ellen, and Margaret Anne, with ourselves made a lively party. They were all warmhearted, interesting people. Jim too had grown up in an affectionate, loyal family whose fundamental standards were much like my own family's. They had very different personalities, and I could easily imagine that when the Randall children were growing up, they also constituted a "little republic, usually verging on anarchy."

I was told about an incident which happened when Jim was a tiny boy. A young preacher, who was evidently lacking in warm understanding, was calling. He began to scold Jim's mother for not always attending the church meetings, not taking into account the fact that a woman with four small children to care for cannot always get away from home. She showed she was hurt and her little son was furious with the self-righteous visitor. Squaring himself in front of the man and wiggling one small finger belligerently, the spirited four-year-old said, "I could lick you with my little finger!" The scolding ended abruptly as the embarrassed preacher took his departure without delay!

Mary and her husband lived with Mother Randall. Alice and Arthur had attractive homes in a suburb, Irvington. There were family suppers at each of these houses, and I wrote in my diary: "Jim and I inspected both homesteads and I was especially interested in Jim's paintings." I had not realized before that he had done as many watercolors and oils as I saw on the walls. He had not had training in art but the instinct of the artist was strong within him, especially for making portraits. I learned from his family how, as a little boy, he had loved to draw the face of Lincoln and had painted Lindoln's head in oils when he was about twelve.

Jim's early interest in Lincoln is evident in another story which his sister Alice told me much later. "In May before his graduation from High School," she wrote, "he was asked to give a talk in our beloved Hall Place Church. I'll never forget that Sunday afternoon! I can see him now standing up there on the platform in a new suit and speaking on his favorite subject—Lincoln!" She added with the deep affection characteristic of the Randall family, "My, but he did look handsome! His older sister was mighty proud of him."

Jim enjoyed making pencil sketches of his friends, often without their knowledge, at public gatherings or just from memory. We were to take our meals at the University Club that summer in Urbana and many a sketch on a three-by-five card was drawn unobtrusively below the level of the table as we sat at meals. In later years we kept a secret file of these portraits which we named the "Rogues' Gallery." Few of the subjects knew they were included!

We arrived in Urbana about the middle of June. Writing here today I find it interesting to read in my diary how this town first appeared to me. On our second

Dr. F. V. N. Painter
By J G Randall
1929

Three Sketches and a Painting by Jim

Jim delighted in sketching and painting in general, and
especially in doing portraits. Above, right, is an oil painting
of Lincoln which he did at the age of twelve; left, a sketch
of Lincoln. Below, sketches of my father and me.

day I wrote: "We walked around the wonderful campus and over into Champaign in evening. This is a beautiful place, every street lined with magnificent trees, mostly elms." (Elm disease was then far in the future.) The blackness of the soil and its fertility amazed me. I remember writing home that this certainly must be the place where Jack grew his beanstalk.

We found Urbana then — and later — a most friendly place. At the University Club we lunched and dined with many people and soon had a congenial circle of friends with whom to go places and do things. Except for the ever-pressing war anxiety, that was a happy summer. I took the Red Cross course in home nursing at the university and we entered fully into all the social activities and entertainments of the summer session. In July I wrote: "Our life here is satisfactory and interesting." We felt more than ever that we wanted Jim to get a position in a large university, not a small college.

But for the immediate future he was extremely anxious to get into war work. The day after we returned to Salem in August he went to Washington to see about a position in the Historical Section of the General Staff. A letter on August 20 told me that the men in charge wanted him but a new ruling kept him out because he was a civilian.

The next two weeks were filled with swift events and an uncertainty which was an intense strain. My emotion is evident in what I wrote in my diary on August 21, our first wedding anniversary: "Each night I thank God for the great gift of my husband, and pray for years of happiness and good together."

Two days later Jim wired me from Washington that he was to be sent on a two-week lecturing engagement in Indiana by the Committee on Public Information. While he was on this trip the offer of an appointment as a Y.M.C.A. secretary came from Washington and a telegram from the Shipping Board calling him to Washington for an interview. I had to forward this telegram to him when I was not sure just where he was. He wired me as soon as he received it and said he would go to Washington directly from Indiana.

In the late afternoon of September 7, "After a day of intense anxiety," I received from Jim the following telegram: "Am appointed on Shipping Board, salary thirty-six hundred a year." He was called a special expert and his title was historian. In a letter next day he told me what his duties were. "When you consider," he wrote, "that every phase of the Shipping Board's activities in the construction, operation, requisitioning of ships, fixing of rates &c. &c. has to be digested in my office and presented in the report, you can see that the job is no snap." This, however, was the position we wanted most, as it did not involve our being separated. It was to be a great change of atmosphere in Jim's work and in our way of life. The college professor and his small-town wife were to live in the maelstrom of our nation's capital when it was engaged in a great war.

Before I could join Jim in Washington I must dismantle the home in Salem which had been built up with such loving enthusiasm. I stored our furniture in the big, all-embracing house of my parents. When I reached Washington several weeks later we began the far greater task of finding a place to live in a city which, because of the war, was crowded almost beyond belief. After days of depressing search we were finally able to get the third floor of a private home, a brick duplex at 1220 Kenyon St. N.W. We paid one hundred dollars a month for two rooms, bath, and an improvised kitchen with a gas stove but no sink or running water. We were extremely lucky, for the owners of the house, Mr. and Mrs. John Murphy, were kind and pleasant and we had the essentials of living.

My diary shows that the days fell into a certain routine. I prepared breakfast and supper at our third-floor apartment but at noon I would join Jim downtown in his office at 1319 F Street N.W. Then we would go out to lunch together and afterwards, according to my diary, we would usually take "a short stroll in the park back of the White House." Sometimes we would steal a bit more time and walk over to the Washington Monument. We were in the very heart of beautiful, historic Washington and loved it.

We were not only in a historic setting; we were living in the midst of dramatic history. The war news had become much more encouraging that fall and when November came in, it was evident that Germany's surrender was near. On the evening of November 4 Jim and I attended a play, and when we came out of the theater, newsboys were crying "Extra — the war is over!" We came home dazed with that thought, not knowing whether to believe it or not. Next day we found it was a false report.

Three days later, when I joined Jim for lunch, I found downtown Washington swarming with crowds and was told Germany had surrendered. Government clerks and soldiers, to quote my diary, "seized every available auto, mail wagon — anything — piled into it and paraded through the streets waving flags and cheering. Bells ringing — whistles blowing." Jim and I took a carriage and drove along the Potomac River and past the Lincoln Memorial for an hour. We came back by the White House, where a huge crowd was assembled. Then in the evening we heard the news was again a mistake.

Several days later I was awakened in the middle of the night by a crying in the streets. As the mists of sleep cleared away, I recognized that it was newsboys once more calling that the war was over. Was this another false report? Morning brought the news that Germany had signed the armistice. I wrote in my diary, "I simply can't realize it." It seemed too wonderful to be true, that the great, black, menacing cloud of war which had hung over us for so long, disrupting and darkening our lives, was at last lifted, that there would be no more wounding and killing, that people could now return to the sweet normal way of living for which they had hungered for so long. I joined Jim downtown and we sat in a front window of the Munsey Building for quite a while watching the parades and celebration on Pennsylvania Avenue. The streets, says my diary, "were like 4th of

July, Hallowe'en and New Year's Eve all in one." My
account for November 11, 1918, ends: "This is truly the
greatest day yet recorded in my diary."

The next evening we went to Keith's vaudeville to
celebrate. As we neared the entrance, a group of police-
men appeared and cleared a lane through the crowd with
their outstretched arms. For a moment I felt indignant at
finding myself barricaded by a powerful arm and then I
saw President and Mrs. Woodrow Wilson passing by to
enter the theater. They were so close I could almost have
touched them.

Newspaper headlines about the war were far less
prominent now, but news about another disaster was
replacing them. The terrible influenza epidemic of 1918
had broken out that fall and was getting steadily worse.
The column of death notices in the papers grew longer
and longer. Keith's now had a sign on the door saying, if
I remember correctly, that it was closed until "the flu
has flown." Public gatherings were being canceled.
There was no more room in the hospitals. Two of our
friends died in that epidemic.

We took what precautions we could. We always
gargled with an antiseptic mouthwash when we had
been out. For a time I prepared a lunch for Jim to take
to his office with him, so that he would not have to go
into the crowded restaurants.

Christmas approached but we did not dare take a trip
as we had planned. This would be my first Christmas
away from home. I had had another of my throat
infections early in the month and was still under the

weather on December 24. I asked Jim to go to market for me, giving him a list and adding as an afterthought, "You might bring back a small duck to roast."

What he brought back for the two of us was a nine-and-a-half-pound goose! We spent the afternoon roasting it together, as we were invited out for Christmas Day itself. First I got out my cookbook and read aloud to Jim the directions which began: "Wash the goose thoroughly." I went on reading aloud, and when I looked up, Jim had a bar of kitchen soap and a brush and was scrubbing that goose with all his might. It was probably the most thoroughly washed goose in culinary history! We could barely get it into the broiler pan of our little oven and we took turns basting it every fifteen minutes. We had so much fun that all feeling of homesickness vanished. The goose had saved the day. When it was roasted a beautiful brown, Jim proudly brought out his Christmas present to me, a Sheffield silver platter with a well and tree, and we triumphantly placed our roast goose upon it. Ever afterwards that holiday was, for us, the Christmas of the Roast Goose.

The Shipping Board was busy bringing our soldiers home from Europe, so Jim's work with them continued through the first half of 1919. On February 27 we witnessed another historic event, the "Welcome Home" parade on Pennsylvania Avenue. It was led by President Wilson walking briskly with uplifted face and triumphantly carrying the American flag. He was followed by hundreds of soldiers and endless army equipment. In its scope this parade could be compared to that of the Union Army after the Civil War.

Events and friendships in Washington grew increasingly interesting that spring. We attended the leading plays and heard famous men lecture. I can close my eyes now and see John Galsworthy as he read from his own works with his lovely wife seated near him on the platform. He told of a pet dog whom they had loved even as I had loved Laddie, and when he came to their sorrow over losing this precious member of the family, I could hardly wipe my tears away fast enough. I sniffed and wept all the way home, with Jim, somewhat embarrassed, doing his best to comfort me.

With the war over, our thoughts turned to getting back into academic life. Jim received offers from Ohio Wesleyan University, Butler College, and Syracuse University that year, declining them all. One trouble was that academic salaries had not caught up with the soaring cost of living. When his war work ended in July, Richmond College was offering him a professorship at three thousand dollars and he accepted it, though it was not the position in a big university which we both wanted. He went ahead of me to Richmond, where once more he was faced with Peter's dilemma of having a wife and no place to keep her. There had been little building during the war and the demand for houses and apartments far exceeded the supply.

In the end we were forced to buy a small house in Richmond at 1810 Floyd Avenue. Since Richmond College was in Westhampton, this meant that Jim must take a considerable walk as well as a considerable streetcar ride to get to his classes. This arrangement was far from satisfactory and we missed being in a faculty community close to the college. We also soon found that with his heavy teaching load and this time-consuming commuting, he could not get ahead with his writing.

That winter of 1919–1920 was saddened for us by the long illness of Jim's mother and her death from cancer. We went to Indianapolis at Christmas to see her, a heartbreaking experience. When we returned I got chilled before we could get the cold house adequately heated again and became ill with a throat infection which flared up, off and on, until summer came.

There were, however, bright features of our year in Richmond. It is a city rich in historic interests and full of lovely people. We formed a cherished friendship there with one of the most sparkling and lovable personalities we had known, Evan R. Chesterman. He was a newspaperman and author who had become badly crippled with arthritis. Mrs. Chesterman for a while served dinners to a privileged number of paying guests, Jim and myself among them, and we spent many happy evenings with the interesting group who gathered around that long table at 1636 West Grace Street. Mr. Chesterman presided over it with rare wit and humor and a literary flair that made it a delight to be present.

One thing Jim enjoyed especially at Richmond was the high quality of his students. He was devoted to them and they to him. When we left Richmond College they gave him a silver pitcher on which was engraved: "Presented to Dr. J. G. Randall by his classes, 1920." In the ceremonious presentation they described him as "a most able teacher, a professor interested in student activities and a friend of all the students."

Jim taught in the summer session at Butler College that summer and in September he went to the University of Illinois. Much as we had loved being there in the summer of 1918, it was a difficult decision for him to accept an assistant professorship at a salary of twenty-five hundred dollars when at the same time he had two offers from Washington at four thousand dollars — one from the Shipping Board, which wanted him back, and the other of a position as historian in the Air Service.

I had acquired a taste for living in the nation's beautiful capital, which was so much nearer my parents than Illinois, and shortsightedly wanted us to return to Washington. I have never ceased to be thankful that Jim had the wisdom to take the long-range view and establish us where we belonged, in a large university. Our wartime odyssey was now ended. Our friendly providence apparently had a hand in this critical decision, for Illinois, which would henceforth be our home, was the land of Lincoln.

8.

Diary Portrait of Days at 1101 West Oregon Street

Jim went to Urbana ahead of me to start his teaching in September. My father took us to the familiar station in Salem where I watched the train pull out and disappear in the distance. That night I wrote in my diary, "I do not know exactly when I shall follow," adding that I had to wait until Jim found a place for us to live.

This proved a most discouraging task. It was impossible for him to get housekeeping quarters and, after considerable delay, he took the same two rooms with bath in a private home which we had occupied during the summer session two years before. This plan involved our taking all our meals at the University Club.

By that time I had become ill again. In the end it seemed best, since Jim was coming east in December anyway to attend a meeting, for me to remain in Salem until he could join me at the holidays. Thus it came about that we had one more cherished Christmas in the old home with my father and mother, trimming their tree for them with the ornaments dear to me since I was a child. After Christmas we went to Washington for the meeting of the American Historical Association, which was always exciting in its reunion with friends and its exchange of news and ideas. January of 1921 found us in our two rooms at 806 West California Street, Urbana. All our happy years at Illinois now lay before us, each with its gifts of joy, plus the usual allotment of trials which is common human experience.

For the next three years I have no guiding diaries to go by in telling our story, only letters. In my illness the fall before I had let my diary lapse and it was in January 1924 that Jim first began to keep a day-by-day record of our life together. He put almost everything into his diaries, all the events, the names of people who came into our lives, what these people talked about, and his own comments. The diaries even have a few headlines and illustrations – pasted-in pictures and once in a while a little sketch. His sense of fun frequently crops up; indeed, all his qualities do, for no man can write such a diary without thoroughly revealing himself. Anyone reading these diaries can practically move in and live with the Randalls.

The diaries make clear the pattern of our lives. They give a rounded-out picture of how pleasant life in a university community is, with one's chosen work, congenial friends, informal get-togethers, and public entertainments such as plays, concerts, lectures by famous men, and football games. In the last category I find, in

the very first diary, the record of a famous event in
sports. On October 18, 1924, Illinois played Michigan
in the new Illinois stadium. Jim's record reads: "The
crowd went wild over the spectacular plays of [Red]
Grange who caught the ball on the first kick-off & ran
95 yards for a touchdown. He also made 4 other
touchdowns in a game which netted a score of 39 (Ill.)
to 14 for Michigan."

As I watched that first long, fleet run, I had a feeling
that this could not be real. Of course we were constantly
jumping up and down and this added another kind of
excitement for me. Because the stadium was not quite
complete we sat in temporary seats and Jim's seat was at
the end of a row with no railing to protect him from a
drop of about ten feet. Every time we jumped up I made
a grab for him, fearing he, in his excitement, would step
off the edge.

By the time Jim began his first diary, we had moved
into a five-room apartment at 1101 West Oregon Street
which was to be our address for many, many years. It
was an ideal location, about two blocks from the campus
and close to the University Club, where we still went
frequently for lunch or dinner. Most of our friends were
within easy walking distance. Two couples, Avery and
Grace Craven and Arthur and Minnie Drucker, lived
only a few blocks away; Albert and Cleta Olmstead just
around the corner.

Urbana was a little town then whose Main Street was
not very different from the sleepy Main Street in Salem.
When we first knew them, the twin towns of Cham-

paign and Urbana together had a population of approximately thirty thousand and the university about seventy-five hundred students, not counting those at the professional colleges in Chicago. These figures seem ridiculous today in view of the enormous increase in both.

In addition to the five rooms the apartment had a pleasant little porch opening off the living room. It was on the first floor, but some years later we moved upstairs to the apartment over it and the porch then was surrounded by the branches of the magnificent elms in front of the building.

To a stranger entering the apartment I think the first impression would have been one of color and books. On the living room floor was the rich red Khiva Bokhara rug which had been our one extravagance when we were married, and the walls of the study which adjoined it were lined with bookcases. In the study was Jim's desk, which, as a friend said when he bought it, was "big enough to write a history of the world on." This desk was usually piled up with manuscripts and books in an untidy fashion, for the study was definitely a scholar's workshop. The other furnishings were modest and somewhat haphazard, for we were both rather happy-go-lucky housekeepers.

Reading Jim's diaries today I get a number of surprises. I had not read them before except when he showed me some special passage, usually one which he had put in to tease me. One thing stands out strongly in all of them: that his profession of teaching and writing always came first and that he worked very hard at both. He would come home from his classroom lectures, to which he always gave his best effort, and then endeavor to write a few more pages in his current manuscript. I cannot think of any record which shows more clearly than these diaries the struggle of a professor who is trying to be a good teacher and at the same time produce significant scholarly books.

We made the usual sacrifices for his work. Though we needed the money, Jim did not again teach in the University of Illinois summer school, because he wanted the time for his research and writing. (Later, offers for summer teaching came from other distinguished universities which we could not resist.) In those earlier years he usually went to Washington in the summer for his research while I stayed economically at Salem with my father and mother.

Though he had had a raise in salary, his first diary shows graphically that we were still on a restricted budget in 1924. The entry for February 25 has the heading, "Four more days till Pay Day." On February 26 it was "three more days till Pay Day," and so on until February 29, which has a triumphant caption in large letters, "PAY DAY."

The illustration for this is a small drawing showing accumulated bills skewered on what we always called "the billery." There are glimpses of parts of the bills showing such phrases as "Please remit," "In account with," "Due $12.98," and the like. We made a light-hearted game of our economies and were looking forward happily, as young couples do, to the time when Jim's books would bring him fame and fortune. A passage from a letter which he wrote me in June of this same year makes a pleasant conclusion to this paragraph. The letter begins "EXTRA!" and tells of his raise in rank and "a salary of $3500."

Another illustration was one he showed me at the time and we laughed over it together. On April 21 the entry begins, "Ruth & I had a discussion concerning our vacation plans today." The picture is a clipping which advertises a play. It shows two stormy profiles, those of an actor and actress, engaged in what was evidently a most vehement argument, their noses almost touching!

Plans for vacations presented problems on which we were likely to have different points of view. Jim did not consider any vacation worthy of the name which did not include strenuous hiking, swimming and boating, and I could not keep up with him. Early in our marriage I had learned what Jim's idea of a hike was. It was our first April together and we had gone out to the Virginia woods to gather wild flowers. I wearily recorded in my diary that night: "In afternoon took a hike after Jim's own heart — going over 7 or 8 barb wire fences, several brooks, plowed fields and up and down the whole way." At that time he would sometimes go with friends on all day hikes of sixteen or seventeen miles.

We usually managed to work out some compromise about our vacations. We both liked to fish, fortunately, and we spent many hours trolling, I holding the fishing rod in the back of the boat while Jim rowed. I shall never forget the thrill of our catching what was my first real fish. It was at beautiful Mountain Lake in Virginia. When I felt a sudden, fierce strike on the end of the line, I got so excited I cried out, "A big one! A big one!" and fairly threw the rod at Jim. He grabbed it and, while I held my breath in suspense, skillfully reeled in what I was sure was the handsomest black bass ever caught.

We soon found the pleasantest plan for vacations was to go with members of Jim's family, in which case the men could lead the strenuous life while their wives kept house in a lakeside cottage.

Each picture in the diaries seems connected with a story. I was brought up short by another one in this first diary. In February Jim had been sick in bed with the flu for several days and consequently had not shaved. He had grown a flourishing but most unbecoming stubble of dark beard. I made a pencil sketch of his face thus adorned, and unknown to me he had pasted it in his diary. The mention of flu brings up one of the worst of our allotted "trials." In the winter months we were both extremely susceptible to colds and flu. I used to say ruefully that if either one of us saw a flu germ halfway down the block, he would run to meet it!

To sum up what Jim's diaries reveal, one might consider what would have been seen by that hypothetical person who moved in with the Randalls by way of reading these diaries. He could have watched them day by day. He could have seen the Mr. hurrying through breakfast in order to make his eight-o'clock class and the

Mrs. busy with her morning chores, not minding that her husband had left the cap off the toothpaste and failed to shut the bureau drawer after getting out a clean shirt. Later in the day the invisible visitor might have witnessed the two conferring over a manuscript in the study, the wife doing such tasks as checking references, transferring corrections to carbon copies, and possibly making some suggestions. Sometimes she was asked to read an article or book and make notes on it, and always the husband would record "Ruth's help" in his diaries.

The apartment knew its ups and downs. There were worried faces in times of illness and occasional clashes of nerves. Sometimes the imaginary observer might have heard spirited arguments about matters other than vacations. Often the dispute was about some such subject as the Mr. wearing his raincoat or rubbers or, on vacations, taking a dip before breakfast in a chilly lake. It was after such a cold dip at Mountain Lake that he had developed a severe throat infection, but had the typical masculine reaction to a wife's protective measures.

There were occasions which showed how the husband loved to entertain their friends. One diary gives an account of a party on his birthday, June 24. By afternoon the apartment was straightened up and the table, in the dining room with its blue and cream Chinese rug, was festive with flowers. The host's face glowed as he welcomed his guests and, when all was ready, he liked to usher them to the table by saying, "Let's go from the red room to the blue room." Here is his diary account: "In the eve'g we had a little birthday party, with the Olmsteads, Druckers & Cravens. We played kid games & cut two birthday cakes. Ruth used her silver cake knife for the first time since our wedding. We all had a delightful time & the occasion showed us how very much our dear friends mean to us here."

After the party the host and hostess would wash the dishes together, he washing, she wiping and putting away, while they talked over what a nice evening it had been.

The imaginary visitor might have seen the Randalls in winter bundling up to go on one of their cherished "snow hikes." Both loved the thrill of walking through a white, transfigured world with the big flakes pelting down around them. They shared the magic of what Stephen Vincent Benét has called its "changed and luminous light." And in summer the couple might have been found sitting on their little porch in quiet companionship, talking over the day's events and making future plans. They had invented a word for these restful periods: they were, they said, "quietizing."

And finally the invisible observer might have noticed that the two saved the letters they had written to each other. They were letters full of their mutual interests and passages of deep affection. Let one passage, which the husband wrote to his wife several years after their marriage, stand for them all: "The sweetness of our married life is the chief thing in life to me."

The years slipped by rapidly, one dissolving into another as scenes sometimes do in movies. One memorable event of 1925 was my parents' golden wedding anniversary on August 9. That week daughters, husbands, and children kept arriving at the big white house on High Street in Salem until, as Jim wrote in his diary, it was "necessary to rent three cots so that we could all sleep under the same roof." Only my brother's and Laura's families could not come. "Bedding down" the crowd on the night of August 8 was the occasion of much hilarity. Jim recorded, "Ruth & I called our quarters 'lower ten' while Henry Jr. said he was sleeping in the 'caboose.' "

There was futher merriment on the morning of August 9 when Henry Hanson, Sr., presented the "bride" first with a number of ludicrous gifts such as a toy auto and a popgun, and then with a great bouquet of golden roses and the gold wristwatch which her daughters were giving her. At dinner the table was extended to its utmost limit for fourteen members of the family. Jim had his camera loaded and took pictures, including one of my father and mother that we always treasured. That afternoon old friends kept calling. It was a loving celebration.

But it was the last gathering of the clan in the old home in Salem. My parents had grown frail and needed to be near one of their children. A few months later they bought a house next door to my sister Margaret in Marion, Virginia, and moved there.

For us the biggest event of 1926 appears under a huge diary headline on September 22: "THE BOOK ARRIVES." It was *Constitutional Problems Under Lincoln* and Jim's first book aside from his thesis. Only he and I

Their Golden Wedding Day

Jim took this picture of my father and mother in front of the old home where they had lived the whole fifty years. My mother is holding a bouquet of golden roses.

knew the infinite pains and the endless labor which had gone into its making. That evening we walked over to the Cravens' and found them ready to celebrate the event with a gay ceremony. They put on a coronation scene for Jim, as his diary records, "with a throne, a paper crown, an impressive salute, and such other 'foolishment' as the occasion demanded."

During the time he was completing this book Jim was also doing editorial work in collaboration with Professor Theodore Pease on the diary of Orville H. Browning, a close friend of Lincoln's. I find frequent references during this period too, to our working together on that fascinating mystery called "The Diary of a Public Man," which had been published in four installments in the *North American Review* in 1879. It had close-up material about Lincoln and other public figures in Washington early in the Civil War. The mystery was, who wrote it? Research on it had all the charm of a jigsaw puzzle and we worked hard and enthusiastically at it, piecing together little clues contained within it. In the end, however, Jim found he could not prove who the diarist was and he withheld his research from publication.

The year after the first book's appearance I was quite ill with a stubborn kidney infection. It was clear we needed some household help, for it was too hard on Jim to carry his work and prepare our meals too. He was cheerfully ready to undertake cooking but his zeal exceeded his know-how, and his culinary attempts sometimes had unexpected results. Thereby hangs a family story. Once when I was out for the afternoon he decided to surprise me by having dinner ready when I returned. His menu included, according to his diary, some "fine country sausage" which he fried, and then it occurred to him to make some gravy. He remembered that he had seen me stir flour into the grease left in the pan. He began to look for the flour and after a search found it (as he thought) and stirred some of it in. When it did not thicken as he expected he added more "flour." The mixture kept bubbling up as he continued to add more and more of the white stuff, until he realized that something was wrong. He pulled the skillet from the fire, and as the concoction cooled, it solidified into what looked exactly like butterscotch candy. He had been putting in powdered sugar! He tasted it, declared it was good, and gleefully named his invention "sausage scotch."

The decision to have some domestic help brought into our lives two very fine personalities. Both had the instinctive wisdom and understanding which I had known in our beloved "Aunt Mary" when I was a little girl. The first was May Evans, a woman of keen intelligence who taught me many things about cooking and housekeeping in general. When she could no longer come to us, we were able to get Caroline Woodruff, who was to prove a great blessing to us for many, many years. We both loved her as if she were a member of the family. With her help we could have friends in to dinner more often and Caroline's fried chicken and hot biscuits became famous among them.

May Evans was our helper in the spring of 1927 when Jim wrote the following headline in his diary: "DR. &

MRS. PAINTER VISIT US." To the delight of us all, my parents were making the round of all their children, visiting first my brother and his family at the University of Texas in Austin, then Laura and hers at the University of Oklahoma in Norman, us at the University of Illinois, and Julia and Arch at Western Reserve University in Cleveland. From Cleveland the Throckmortons would drive them to Gettysburg College to visit the Hansons. (The list of universities shows why I sometimes say my family is "all cluttered up with professors"!)

In the days my parents were with us, Jim's diary fairly glows with his pleasure in having them. They met our friends and we did the things we knew they would like, including reading aloud in the evenings. We felt bereft when we finally had to take them to their train to continue their parental pilgrimage. Jim, of course, took them into their car and seated them, which took some minutes. I, who had remained outside, could see the conductor impatiently waiting to give the signal for the train to start, so I said to him, "Don't you go off with my husband!" I promptly received this jovial retort: "Oh, you'd have no trouble getting another!" Jim, when he heard of this, was so amused that he wrote it in his diary. He also recorded that their visit "has been perfect." My father, he said, "looked 100% better than when he arrived" and my mother was "sweeter & finer than ever."

Jim's publications were now bringing him offers of summer teaching away from Illinois. He accepted such

an offer that summer at the University of Chicago,
where he had taken his Ph.D. degree. Summer teaching
meant that for a time he would become a member of
another history department, make many new friends, and
be welcomed and entertained as a visiting professor. We
both loved the pleasures and stimulation of such summer
appointments.

In October that year we helped celebrate another
wedding anniversary, the silver anniversary of Jim's
brother Arthur at Indianapolis. It was a heartwarming
occasion on which Jim saw many old friends and talked
of old times, and we were in a mood of happy satisfaction when we took the local train back to Urbana. Jim
remarked in his diary that we made the journey home
"in the full glory of October's finest weather."

It was on another fine autumn day that our trip on
that local train resulted in one of our lighthearted household "pomes." We passed a long line of clothes hanging
on a line. The wind was blowing and some of the
garments filled out and seemed so very much alive that
we had a good laugh over the comic antics of a pair of
pants. Jim used the expressions "the dance of the pants"
and "the flip and the flirt of a skirt." The next day I
wrote some singsong verses embodying these phrases and
gave the jingle the title "From a Train Window." Jim
referred to it as "Poetry on Pants."

> *A car at the station, billboard information,*
>   *A three-color shaving soap sign,*
> *A lone country store with a dog by the door,*
>   *Glide by in the autumn sunshine.*

A weed-bordered road, school bus with a load,
  Goldenrod and a tangle of vine,
And for humor and action, and gay satisfaction,
  The dance of the clothes on a line.

The flip and the flirt of a slip and a skirt
  Made an airy fandango design;
A coy little gown fluttered next to the clown,
  The pants in a dance on the line.

The next summer Jim taught at Duke University in Durham, North Carolina. We rented a house at 1030 West Trinity Avenue, a quaint house which had been built at a time when it was considered improper for a gentleman to see a lady's ankles. So the railing to the stairway, which went up from the living room, was built of solid boards to prevent any such impropriety!

Jim recorded our impressions: "We are charmed with Durham & the people here." We realized, he said, that we were in the South. We enjoyed the cordiality of everyone, the soft speech, and "the leisurely human atmosphere." Even the dogs, he said later, barked "with a Southern accent!" The summer worked out so satisfactorily on both sides that he was asked to return the following summer for the first term of the summer school. That experience was equally delightful. I shall mention only one of the new friendships we made at Durham. When the first term was ended, there appeared an engaging young man who was to teach American history in the second term. We took him out to dinner and were simply charmed with him. His name was Henry Steele Commager.

Sandwiched between these two summer appointments at Duke was the winter of 1928–1929, which we spent in Washington on sabbatical leave from Illinois. Jim went there, as he said, to do research for writing a constitutional history of the United States.

We know from the first chapter of this book that it was fate's design to make him an outstanding Lincoln scholar. His first book included both Lincoln and the Constitution. Was he going to make the wrong turn in the road here by continuing in constitutional study instead of the study of Lincoln? It has been fascinating to me to trace in his diaries the various incidents and factors by which providence detached him from his projected constitutional history and made Abraham Lincoln the great, absorbing study of his life.

9.

Jim Takes Over
Mr. Lincoln —
and Vice Versa

The earliest factor influencing Jim's course was the intense interest in the face of Lincoln which he felt when he was a small boy. As he drew and painted those features they fascinated and challenged him, as they do most people with an instinct for portraiture. Later, his graduate work had been centered in the Civil War period in which Lincoln was the outstanding figure. The major part of all his writing up to this time had had Lincoln in it.

In October 1927 Jim was writing, for the *Dictionary of American Biography*, the biographical sketch of Salmon P. Chase, who had been in Lincoln's cabinet. Chase had been married three times and six daughters had been born to him. Jim turned over to me the problem of getting all those wives and children into one paragraph without confusion. He asked me to study the subject and write it up for him.

I was greatly interested in doing this. Constitutional history left me cold but I loved writing about real people. I found the collaboration most pleasant. It may be significant that on October 15 Jim wrote in his diary: "After struggling painfully with the Chase article I now find that I like biographical writing. Would like to write a biographical book."

October of 1928 found us in Washington on leave and again Jim confided his state of mind to his diary: "I have been somewhat perplexed as to what my 'next book' should be . . . have been somewhat reluctant to turn out another bk. in const. hist. but this seems to be what is expected of me." Twelve days later: ". . . my mind has been buzzing with other books I might write." He mentioned several possible subjects, including the Emancipation Proclamation, the life of Greeley; and the presidency of Lincoln.

In November I find another straw which shows which way the wind was blowing. He was now definitely investigating what material on Lincoln was available. His diary says, "took occasion to examine the Lincoln mss. at L. of C. [Library of Congress]." From then on he was doing Lincoln research to find out what had been done and what aspects of the subject had been neglected. There was a great mass of writing on Lincoln, but little of it met the standards of a historian and a part of it was made up of myth and legend.

The "straws" continued to pile up. In November Jim

visited the L. C. Handy studio to study the Brady photographs of Lincoln. In December, at the meeting of the American Historical Association, he talked with his former professor, William E. Dodd, about the possibility of his writing a book on Lincoln's presidency. In the spring of 1929, when we visited the Hansons at Gettysburg, he interviewed an elderly photographer, Mr. Tipton, who as a boy had witnessed the Battle of Gettysburg and had been present at Lincoln's Gettysburg Address. When we returned to Washington, we went to the Lincoln museum on Tenth Street, where Jim gazed long at the life mask showing the features he had drawn with such intense care when he was a boy.

By May, Jim was writing two thoughtful Lincoln articles which were later published in the *South Atlantic Quarterly*. Then on May 10 the force which was drawing him irresistibly toward a Lincoln biography received a great impetus. His diary tells the story. He had gone to the office of Allen Johnson, editor of the *Dictionary of American Biography*, to deliver a manuscript, and Mr. Johnson "said he had something to talk with me about & said that he wanted very much to have me do the Lincoln article, that he would be very content to put it in my hands, that he wanted me to do for Lincoln what I had done for Chase &c. &c." Mr. Johnson added that various persons had asked for this prize assignment but he had talked it over with the editor of the *American Historical Review*, Dr. J. Franklin Jameson, and other historians and "they thought I was the one to do it."

Jim was thrilled and so was I. By this time I was

getting tremendously interested in Lincoln myself. We
were at Duke University that summer when Jim's birthday arrived and I gave him a copy of Stephen Vincent
Benét's *John Brown's Body*. We read the whole book
aloud to each other, fairly living over the Civil War in
its pages, and there too we met the tall, lank figure of
Abraham Lincoln whose kindness was "as large and
plain as a prairie wind." We both felt about Benét's
book as Jim wrote in his diary: "There are not many
things in American literature that equal it."

We were back in Urbana when the 1930's came in.
Jim was working on his ten-thousand-word *Dictionary*
article on Lincoln, which had now become an absorbing
project for us both. He made his seminar a Lincoln
seminar and apparently had fired his graduate students
with his own enthusiasm. His desire to write a book on
Lincoln was growing stronger all the time. Then fate
saw fit to interpose a detour.

A headline to his diary entry for April 19, 1930, tells
about it. The headline reads: "HEATH & CO. ASKS ME TO
WRITE A BOOK." The letter concerning this invitation
came from the editor of the Heath New History Series,
Allan Nevins, who was to become to us the kind of
friend Lincoln had in mind when he wrote: "The better
part of one's life consists of his friendships."

The proposed book was to be called *The Civil War
and Reconstruction*, certainly an appropriate subject for
a professor who had been working in Civil War sources
since his graduate-student days. He would still be pursuing his Lincoln study in writing it, for the Civil War

period is also the Lincoln period. Jim expected to finish his Lincoln article for the *Dictionary of American Biography* by the end of the year and would then be free to start on this book. So he signed the contract with D. C. Heath and Company.

He did send in the Lincoln article on schedule. On January 5, 1931, his diary tells that he had received a letter from Allen Johnson, the editor, praising the article and saying it was so "masterly" that he would not shorten it but allow its 15,000 words instead of the specified 10,000. Jim admitted to his diary that the letter gave him "quite a thrill," and needless to say, it gave me one too. Three days later, on January 8 his diary reads as follows: "In my study I wrote about 2300 words on my book — i.e. on the 1st chap. dealing with the South."

Writing has been called a pleasant torture or a torturing pleasure. While the project is all-important to you and you would never think of giving it up, there are times when it makes you groan. Two entries that summer show Jim in a state of mind familiar to any author who has struggled to organize a big and complicated subject. In the midst of a heat wave he recorded on July 30 that he had written 750 words "on my beastly Civil War book." The next day, with the thermometer at 97 degrees, he referred to his writing as "the fiendish task." His diaries, for about six years, give in detail the genesis of a scholar's book: the laborious and ever-continuing research, the number of pages accomplished on certain days, the revisions which were often themselves revised, the checking with the sources, and, in the later stages,

the meticulous reading of the long sheets of galley proof,
then page proof, and the final exhausting effort which is
like a panting racer's terminal spurt of speed, the making
of the index.

Apropos of reading proof Jim later wrote a bit of
doggerel. It is a parody of an old poem called "Horatius"
by Thomas Babington Macaulay. The poem tells how,
in "the brave days of old," the heroic Horatius stood on
the bridge and fought valiantly to keep the invading
enemy from passing over it. Another hero volunteered
to help Horatius, saying he would stand at his right hand
and keep the bridge with him. Imitating the stately and
antiquated language, Jim pictured the harassed professor
as he struggled with the proof:

> *The sweat stood on Professor's brow,*
> *He couldn't make it go.*
> *The more he worked the worse he got,*
> *The proof-sheets laid him low.*
>
> *Then up spake Wife Courageous:*
> *"Don't get into a stew,*
> *For I will sit at your right hand*
> *And read the proof with you."*

Using all the printer's terms he could think of, Jim
gave some of the dialogue of the proofreaders:

> *"Three dots for the ellipsis;*
> *Indent two ems, not three!*
> *How is it in the proof?" he asked.*
> *"It's short one dot," said she.*

"Put Republican in capitals,
Transpose, delete, depress,
Wrong font . . . see copy . . . stet . . . etcet.
Spare the ibid *. . . add an 's.' "*

This effusion, called "Wifey at the Proof," ends triumphantly with the shipping back of the corrected proof sheets and the publication, months later, of the book. On March 20, 1937, Jim wrote, in a very different vein, in his diary: *"Important!* THE BOOK ARRIVES. The expressman brought six copies of 'the book.' Great stir and excitement. Polly nearly kissed the expressman!" (He had long since adopted my family nickname, "Polly.") Of course we had a "jubilee" over it and were further thrilled the next day when the *Illini,* the University newspaper, quoted Allan Nevins as saying the book was "a piece of literary history" which would "at once become standard for the period."

While he had been working on this book, Jim had continued his study of the Civil War President. As early as 1929 he had come to feel about Lincoln, as he wrote in his diary, that "historians have not yet rescued his personality from the myth & fiction with which it is encrusted." This conclusion had grown and matured during his continued research, with the result that in December 1934 he read at the meeting of the American Historical Association a paper whose title asked the question "Has the Lincoln Theme Been Exhausted?" As David C. Mearns, chief of the Manuscripts Division of the Library of Congress, has written, this paper "proceeded systematically, cogently, and convincingly to answer with a thundering negative." The paper made clear the need for further work on Lincoln which would remove the encrustation of myth and fiction, search out unused sources, present as facts only material whose authenticity had been tested by a historian's standards, and show Lincoln as a conscientious scholar found him.

At that same meeting Jim suggested to Paul Angle that they collaborate on a life of Lincoln. Paul agreed and that was the plan for some time. Fate's design for Jim, however, called for him to produce his Lincoln biography alone. In the end Paul Angle found that he had too many other commitments to take on this collaboration.

I must now go back and catch up with other events in the 1930's. The year 1931 brought us a deep sadness. My father had grown increasingly frail and in January we received the news of his death. I felt that one of the strongest foundations of my life had been swept away. Since I was just getting over the flu at the time, I did not attempt the long winter journey to Virginia to attend his funeral.

We intended, of course, to go to see my mother during the coming summer. It would have to be somewhat late in the summer, as for more than a year we had been planning to take a Colorado vacation in July with Jim's sister Alice and her husband. By Sunday, June 14, our reservations and all other preparations were made for starting west on July 4.

That Sunday afternoon I was suddenly overwhelmed with a feeling that we must go to Virginia and see my mother *before* we went to Colorado. It was a feeling of such urgency and apprehension that I could not overcome it. I finally told Jim how I felt and at once he said, "Then we will go. We still have time." On Monday we telegraphed my sister Margaret we were coming, and with hasty preparations we were able to leave Urbana Wednesday morning. We arrived in Marion shortly after noon on Thursday.

Jim's diary records on that day, "We found Mrs. Painter quite well & looking fine." We knew that her heart was not strong and that her activities were very much restricted, but she was extremely glad to see us, and except for the ache of missing my father, it seemed a happy, normal visit. I remember especially bringing her some flowers from her garden and the pleasure she took in arranging them in a bowl.

It was around four o'clock Sunday morning when we were awakened and told she was having a heart attack. Margaret had summoned the local physician and they were doing everything possible to help her. But they could do little except to try to ease her distress. At five-fifteen her labored breathing ceased.

It all happened so suddenly it seemed hard to believe. It was just the Sunday before that I, in Urbana, had felt that urgency to come to see her. I shall never forget how I felt that afternoon as I took from the bowl the wilted flowers that her hands had arranged two days before. Jim, whose tenderness and understanding were my great comfort, wrote in his diary, "Ruth grieves deeply at the loss of her dear little mother."

We were glad we could share with Margaret and her husband, Tumpus, the sad duties of the next several days. We took my mother back to Salem, and there, surrounded by many old friends who shared our sorrow, we saw her buried beside my father. We left them there together in the little town where they had lived happily for so many years, the little town whose name means peace.

As I read Jim's diaries for the 1930's they recall events as vividly as do travel slides when thrown upon a screen. In July after my mother's death we had a healing vacation at the Hewes-Kirkwood Inn, not far from Estes, Colorado. One well-remembered picture in my mind is of driving through tall evergreen trees, higher and higher up the mighty mountainside, and I still feel the thrill I felt when a magnificent stag, his antlered head proudly lifted, dashed across the road in front of our car. Another is of standing at night outside our little cabin in the woods and looking up at the stars. They seemed so close in the crystal air I felt I could almost reach up and pick one out of the sky. Let those two vivid recollections represent our Colorado vacation.

Most of the events and situations during this period were happy ones. It was in 1933 that Caroline Woodruff became our full-time household helper and my invaluable counselor. This meant we could have lunch or dinner guests as frequently as we pleased without undue pressure on me and we both loved to invite our friends in.

I was enjoying a creative outlet in making original rug patterns and hooking them. Jim's interest appears in diary entries like this: "Polly is all keyed up about a 'Virginia rug' she is designing. Very interesting. Oriental pattern." The following year there is another announcement: "Polly has nearly finished the beautiful 'Lincoln rug,' of her own designing." This was a special order. He had expressed a wish for a Lincoln rug for his study and I had been working on it for months.

In spite of living in an apartment we now had the gardener's joy of raising flowers. We rented the backyard of the house next door for this purpose and in the spring each first bloom of tulip or columbine rated headlines in the diaries. In addition to being a pleasure, the gardening seemed to agree with Jim. He had advanced from his weight as a bridegroom (116 pounds, as I remember) to 140 pounds. He was happy in doing the very kind of teaching and writing that he wanted to do. I was greatly interested in his work and tried to help in various ways. I did not know at the time that he regularly recorded my assistance in his diaries. Now, years later, I come upon expressions of appreciation like the following, which was written when he was revising his Civil War manuscript: "Polly is helping me 'like a trump' on the book. Her help is very valuable."

Our prevailing mood in the 1930's is evident in something Jim wrote in his diary when we returned from a happy summer of work, travel, and family visiting:

The Randalls and Their Garden

Jim rented a backyard next door to us on Oregon Street and had a garden. He took this picture of his tulips and me—the tulips came first!

"Polly is purring & singing in & around the jolly old apartment."

I come now to one of our richest sources of pleasure and satisfaction in our academic life. It arose from Jim's warm personal interest in his students. A passage in a letter to me which he wrote shortly after he first came to the University of Illinois, when I was still at Salem, serves to keynote this relationship. In this letter he referred to an assignment he had given one of his classes. The context shows the assignment was of a personal nature, for he said of it: ". . . this will have a good effect, I hope: (1) It will give me a sort of acquaintanceship with the life of the students; (2) It will give the students a chance for self-expression in a way that a history assignment almost never does, and (3) It will be a case of the students doing something of educational value but not primarily for credit. There is too much woodenness in the ordinary relation of teacher & student, I believe."

There was nothing wooden in Jim's attitude toward any student. He always stood ready to listen to any need or problem one of them would present to him and he would go to any length to help. In the nature of the case he came to know his graduate students better than the undergraduate members of a big lecture course. A seminar or his graduate class in historical method would be small enough to meet on occasion in our apartment where he could show them his files of research notes and other scholar's paraphernalia. Then we would have a coffee-and-cake hour and get well acquainted.

Sometimes we gave what Jim in his diaries called "one of our young people's parties." Here is the diary record of such a party in the early 1930's. (Incidentally, it shows that no one had more fun than the diarist himself!) "In the evening we had a grand party, made up of students from the Hist. Method Class." The names mentioned include Robert G. Bone, who would always be one of our favorite people. The diary continues: "We played some famous charades: insinuate, paradox, scintillate, vagrant, factotum, dogmatic." The account even tells the hilarious way in which "scintillate" was acted out and ends happily: "The friendship with this class has been unique & altogether delightful." He usually ended by thinking this about most of his classes.

Perhaps we saw more of the graduate students because we lived so close to the campus and Jim did his writing at home. It was easy for his students to drop in to confer with him in his study. Some of them came to make reports, those whom Jim paid by the hour to do certain routine tasks connected with his writing. (Later, the university paid for a research assistant for him, but that was after his Civil War book had been finished.) In *The Civil War and Reconstruction*, under "Acknowledgments," Jim names these students who had done various jobs, large or small, over the six years in which the book was in the making. He thanks Martin P. Claussen "for stout reenforcement in research tasks and library exploration," Alden L. Powell "for similar work," Harry

E. Pratt "for competent assistance in many ways," W. E. Baringer for typing and help in "checking the manuscript," and Eugene M. Braderman for "scholarly assistance in the making of the index."

Jim's diary pictures a day of index-making: "Our apt. was an index factory," he said. "All hands on deck." Two of the above "boys" and Jim and I, each with a section of page proof, were busily preparing index cards, three thousand of them in all, which Jim would later edit. We worked hard but it was fun too. Jim could always infuse gaiety and enthusiasm into a group whether at work or play.

When the Civil War book came out, it was natural that we should invite graduate students to help celebrate the event. Jim's diary does full justice to "the 'book party' — a beautiful dinner for five 'boys' — James, Bone, Baringer, Braderman, Claussen." (Joseph B. James was a graduate student from the South. We were very fond of him, as we were of all these young men.) The diary continues: "After dinner we had some highly animated games — camouflage, categories (including adjectives to describe the index.)" I have forgotten the rules for the game "categories," but vaguely remember it involved selecting a certain category or class and then describing it with adjectives which must all begin with the same letter. One of the categories on this occasion was "historians." It was "a lot of fun," wrote Jim and then added a fact which touched us both very much: "The boys gave Polly 2 doz. gorgeous roses & gave me a copy of *Where the Blue Begins.*"

I think some of his graduate students were quite perturbed in the spring of 1938 when the news leaked out that Duke University had invited Jim to come there permanently. We had loved our two summers at Duke but the boys need not have worried; the Lincoln subject held Jim captive in Lincoln's state of Illinois.

At the end of his diary for that year Jim wrote in summary: "For myself the yr. 1938 has meant travel, Sabbatical, Lincoln research & the launching of a very solid book on Lincoln." His diary of the year before had even given the very day on which he began his life of Lincoln. He wrote his first 1200 words on October 9, 1937, words that would later appear, revised, in Chapter IV of *Lincoln the President*, Volume I, a chapter called "North and South." A years-long, monumental work had begun.

10.

A Cat Named Bambi

January of 1930 had ushered in what might be called the feline era in the Randall household. The prelude to it had really started the fall before when our friend Mrs. Albert Lybyer begged me to adopt a stray kitten she had found wandering around, hungry and homeless, on a cold, rainy November first. I was sympathetic, of course, and impulsively I answered: "Of course I will take it. Why, you are giving me a birthday present! Today is my birthday." Thus unthinkingly I involved us in the joy and bondage of owning a pet.

We named the little gray kitten Judy. Under care and petting she proved to have an engaging personality, responsive, playful, and full of diverting kitten antics. Jim had an old fur-lined glove which we turned inside out and gave to her and it was fun to watch her pretending to be a hunter, stalking and pouncing upon it unawares. To our delight we realized that the stripes on her forehead made the monogram of the University of Illinois, a capital "I" imposed upon a capital "U."

When the Christmas vacation approached we faced

that perennial problem of the pet owner, what to do with it when you are away. We were to spend Christmas with Jim's people in Indianapolis and he was to go on from there to the meeting of the American Historical Association at Durham, North Carolina. We took Judy to a veterinarian to be cared for while we were gone.

That was certainly our hard-luck Christmas. Jim became ill with the flu and was unable to go to the meeting. He was still very weak and miserable when we returned to Urbana. As soon as we reached our apartment he went to bed while I took a taxi to the veterinarian's to get Judy.

We never knew exactly what had happened, but when I got to the animal hospital Judy was very ill. The veterinarian had been taken sick and she may have been neglected. I carried her home and called another veterinarian, but Judy was too far gone to be helped. The second veterinarian said he thought she had grieved herself to death.

We felt very much distressed about this and missed her at every turn. When we awoke in the mornings there was no little meow at the bedroom door followed by a jump on the bed and an enthusiastic greeting of loud purrs. There was a vacancy for the position of cat in our household. With Jim still miserable from his flu, and zero weather outside, our apartment was filled with gloom.

It was Jim who decided we must get another kitten. We soon discovered it is difficult to find a young kitten in January. Days went by in discouraging efforts to locate one. Some of these efforts had a comic side. I remembered that our friends Professor and Mrs. Sleeter Bull, had a pair of Persian cats, and I phoned her to inquire about the prospect of kittens. I learned that such a prospect was in the indefinite future. "Well, we can't wait until the Bulls have kittens," I said to Jim disconsolately, and it was not until he laughed that I realized how funny that sounded.

Finally Jim put an advertisement in the newspaper. This resulted in our being offered about half of the unwanted cats in Champaign-Urbana! But it did bring a call from a woman who raised red Persian cats, a pleasant, gentle lady named Mrs. Bandy. It was Saturday, January 25, when we went to her home. She had a seven-month-old kitten for sale and at once brought him in from the kennels for our inspection.

We saw a beautiful half-grown cat with a piquant, expressive face which still had that wide-eyed, innocent look which makes kittens so appealing. His auburn fur was long and fluffy, his tail a red-gold plume. I gently put my hand down to him, letting him sniff it, which he did, then courteously rubbed his head against it. Jim took a piece of string from his pocket and trailed it across the floor and the little cat promptly entered into that game with great enthusiasm.

It did not take us long to decide that this was the cat we wanted. Jim wrote a check and received an impressive pedigree which had much repetition of the name Redcoat. We carried the cat home in a grocery carton. When I lifted the lid he leaped out and looked curiously around him at his strange new world. Fearing he might be frightened, I brought out a small rubber ball which had been a plaything of Judy's and rolled it across the floor. The little cat scampered after it, picked it up in his mouth, and brought it back to me. "Oh Jim," I cried excitedly. "We've got a retrieving cat!" It was the first of a number of unusual qualities we were to discover in him.

By evening we had named him Bambi for the young deer in Felix Salten's book of that name. Bambi the fawn had also been born with a "little red coat" and had been very curious about all the things around him. To the new member of our family I was "Missie" and Jim was the "Mister." At bedtime that night Jim wrote in his diary, "The cat is all that could be desired in a pet — well mannered, active & affectionate."

When we awakened in the morning a small furry figure leaped lightly on the bed and came first to me with a little trill which plainly meant "Good morning!" After I had responded and petted him, he crossed over to Jim and greeted him in the same way. The household breathed an air of content. The position of cat had been filled.

We spent Sunday getting better acquainted with our new pet. The day ended with a unique incident. Jim decided to relax with a game of solitaire before going to bed, and since Bambi mewed a polite request to see what he was doing, he picked the cat up and placed him on one corner of the card table where he could watch. As Jim laid down one card upon another here and there, he talked cozily to Bambi about each play he made. Finally he said: "I don't know what move to make next. Show me which card to play, Bambi." Bambi hesitated a moment, then daintily picked up the eight of clubs with his teeth and laid it on another card. We could hardly believe our eyes. Jim wrote delightedly in his diary for that date, "It's a card-playing cat!"

Bambi, however, never again played a card, though he did not lose interest in cards. If we were playing rummy, anagrams, or any other game, he always wanted to be on a corner of the table so that he could watch.

When Jim left to go to his classes Monday morning, Bambi gave his first little cry of distress as he saw the front door close behind him. It was evident he did not want his Mister to leave.

That same morning the phone rang and I heard again the pleasant voice of Mrs. Bandy. The conversation, as I remember it, ran like this:

"How's the kitty?"

"Fine," I answered. "We've named him Bambi. We are delighted with him."

She questioned me closely. "Does he seem contented? Will he eat? Does he cry?"

"He seems very happy and he loves to eat," I replied. "The only time he has cried was when he saw my husband leave this morning."

Mrs. Bandy gave a sigh of relief and said she was so glad. Then she told me the story. Bambi had been the smallest of the litter and had not sold in the fall when the larger kittens had. In December she had given him to a young girl who said she wanted him in spite of the fact that her mother feared and hated cats. After Christmas the girl asked to return him. She said he would not eat but roamed around the house crying in a distressed manner and was unmanageable. It was her opinion no one could make a pet of him.

"Perhaps I should have told you this before," continued Mrs. Bandy, "but when I saw you and your husband playing with him, I felt sure it would be all right. All the cat needed was an owner who would love and understand him." She added that if he was not satisfactory she would take him back and return the check. She did not want to sell us a problem cat.

"I suspect the problem in this case was the mother who was afraid of cats," I said. "Anyway, you couldn't have him back now at any price."

Later, when I understood Bambi's sensitive, high-strung temperament more fully, I could see what a misfit he must have been in that household. He could not adjust to the antagonistic atmosphere of a home whose mistress objected to him. If he was ever pushed around, insecurity and fear would make him scratch and fight.

To us he was the most companionable cat we had ever known. One week after we got him, Jim, noticing how Bambi would follow me from room to room, wrote in his diary that the cat was "getting quite a crush on the lady of the house." As I did my household chores in the mornings, he showed great interest in everything and wanted to "help" me. When I made the bed with his "assistance," it took twice as long! He would dart under the covers as I pulled them up and I had to stop and tickle the interesting-looking bulge that resulted. When I washed dishes at the sink, he would jump up on a shelf from which he could watch the swirling suds. Water held great interest for him and he plainly found the kitchen and bathroom the most entertaining rooms in the apartment. He would watch with complete fascination when either Mister or Missie took a bath.

Sometimes we were even in competition for Bambi's "assistance." Once when I was in the kitchen and the cat was on Jim's desk absorbed in watching the dancing of the typewriter keys, I called "Bambi!" Jim's voice from the study answered: "He can't come now; he's helping me!"

We did not realize at first how unerringly Bambi sensed our moods and feelings. In June after we got the cat Jim received a telephone call telling him he had been promoted to a full professorship. We had looked forward to that promotion for a long time and, of course, we embraced each other and were excitedly expressing our joy when Jim suddenly exclaimed, "Look at Bambi!" The cat was walking around us in circles, arching his back proudly and rolling out his loudest purrs. Of course we petted and praised him for joining us in our celebration.

I have a cherished picture which illustrates how Bambi on another occasion entered into Jim's mood. The incident happened in the early 1930's, the years of a great financial depression. To us the depression meant two cuts in salary and the closing of our bank, but for many

Bambi with His "Mister" and "Missie"

Above, Jim was busy and did not want to pose for his picture that morning. Bambi sensed this and got as close to Jim as he could to lend his support. Here they are, both glaring at the photographer with the same expression! Below, Bambi was quite willing to pose with Missie for the society page of a newspaper.

it swept away their means of making a living. One local photographer, having few or no customers, decided to phone various professors and suggest that he take their pictures in their own homes. Jim had no wish to have his picture taken, but, realizing that the photographer needed help, he agreed to have him come.

The man arrived on a morning in which Jim had planned to catch up on his writing. Preparations for taking the picture such as adjusting the camera and lights consumed much time, and all the while Jim was feeling more and more impatient. Bambi sensed this and climbed on the living room table, getting as close as possible to his Mister to give him moral support. When the proofs came, there they were together, both glaring at the photographer with the very same expression!

At mealtime it soon became our custom to place a chair for Bambi at the dining table. He had good table manners and would sit contentedly between us, daintily accepting any tidbits which came his way. If the expected tidbit was too long delayed, however, he would put up his paw and pat the top of the table to get our attention. Out of this I taught him a little trick called "Press the button." When he was in the right position I would indicate the spot where the button was supposed to be and say, "Press the button for service, Bambi." He would promptly lift his paw and press the spot, whereupon he would receive a little bite of meat as a reward.

Another trick grew out of his habit of retrieving. He had the usual toys, a ball and a catnip mouse, but his most cherished plaything was a floppy piece of leather,

tied to the end of a long string, which we called the
"dingbat." If Jim would throw the dingbat up on top of
a bookcase, Bambi delighted to go up after it. It took
three leaps—to davenport, filing case, and top of bookcase—to get to it. He would then take the three jumps
down carrying the dingbat in his mouth and, with a little
trill of triumph, return it to Jim.

I confess we frequently inflicted a small cat show,
consisting of these two acts, on our long-suffering
friends. A gentleman from another university who was
visiting Urbana once told me a story which seemed to
me to be decidedly pointed. He said he and his wife
wanted to get better acquainted with a new faculty
couple who had a cat, but so far, after making two calls,
they had succeeded only in getting better acquainted
with the cat! If our friends thought the Randalls were
positively fatuous about their cat, we did not blame them.
We admitted it!

Bambi received no reward for going through his acts
for company except our praise. He dearly loved us to
tell him what a beautiful, good, intelligent cat he was.
The more we piled up the complimentary adjectives, the
better he liked it. His face would light up and, to our
great amusement, assume an expression which was almost smug.

Occasionally we had to scold him for such things as
sharpening his claws on our upholstered furniture. We
would say "no," and "bad," with great emphasis. He
well understood what we meant and hated those two
words with his whole feline soul. His ears would go back

at the first sound of them. But in praise lay our means of managing him. We could flatter him into doing almost anything we wanted.

In one incident which we loved to tell about, there was an out-and-out clash of wills between Bambi and ourselves. It arose from the fact that we decided one summer to have a box of pink petunias on our little balcony porch. Bambi took great interest in seeing the box installed and we should have realized what an attraction that long box of earth and green things had for him. The first time we went out he dug a hole in one corner of it.

When we came back to discover this he was promptly informed that digging in that box was "No! No!" The effect of this lasted for a while but soon the temptation proved too much and he dug up several more petunias. This time reproof was sharper; I used the word "bad" with considerable emphasis. Some time later Jim headed off another feline excavation. Then we made the mistake of leaving the porch door open that night and by morning the porch box looked very ragged indeed.

I ordered a fresh supply of petunia plants and set them out, telling Bambi in no uncertain tones to let them alone. But as soon as I was busy elsewhere, he dug up half a dozen of them. Then I did what I had never done before, I spanked him. It was a light spanking, but that made no difference to him. He was outraged because I had insulted his catly dignity.

Bambi waited until Jim and I went out to lunch and then he dug that porch box up from end to end. He would show us! The fury of his digging was evident in the fact that dirt had been thrown out all over the porch. When we returned to the chaos, Bambi was sulking under the bed, looking very angry and unhappy.

Jim and I sat down in the living room to talk over our problem. "I guess we will have to give up our plan for having a porch box," I said.

"Wait," said Jim. "If we could soothe his hurt feelings by praising him and then get the idea across that we have confidence in him and expect him to leave the petunias alone, it might help." He added whimsically, "In other words, try the honor system."

We decided to see if this would work. First Jim went after more petunias while I cleaned up the mess. In an hour or so the porch, complete with blooming plants, was in order.

Bambi had emerged from under the bed but was still registering resentment in every hair. When I picked him up, he stiffened and struggled but I carried him to the porch and placed him, with pointed confidence, right beside the porch box. Then Jim and I sat down in the porch chairs and, without looking at him, we began to talk about him. He was such a beautiful cat, we agreed, and so good and intelligent. We repeated little stories about him which we frequently imposed upon our friends, how once when a bat got into our apartment in the night and hid in a closet, Bambi showed us just where he was, and how another time, he caught a starling which had come down the chimney and brought it straight to Missie. Only a good and intelligent cat, we said, could do things like that. We really laid it on!

When Jim and I had finished our act, I looked at Bambi. All the defiance was gone and he looked relaxed and happy. I petted him then and he made a soft sound in his throat in response.

Was it a promise? I cannot know about that, but I do know that he never again put a paw into the porch box. Apparently the honor system worked!

The first December Bambi was with us we discovered that he added lots of fun to our Christmas. He took a lively interest in the Christmas tree and delighted in slapping the shiny ornaments that hung on it. (We soon learned to put our best ornaments high up out of his reach.) Christmas brought things in boxes, and boxes are a feline specialty. Once I made the mistake of leaving a present half unwrapped while I answered the phone. When I returned Bambi had completed the unwrapping, clawed out the sweater which the box contained (much to its detriment), and was proudly sitting in the box himself.

That first Christmas I put Bambi's gifts—mainly a new catnip mouse—into a small stocking and hung it on the tree. Jim's diary describes what followed: "Bambi had the true Xmas spirit," he wrote. "He found his stocking, pulled it down, unwrapped the gifts & played with them as gleefully as a child."

In time a cat motif appeared in some of our presents. My sister Julia sent me a number of antique milk-glass plates with three little kittens embossed on each one. We acquired a vase and an ashtray ornamented with little cat figures, and several cat books. One Christmas Jim gave me Oliver Herford's slim little volume called *The Rubaiyat of a Persian Kitten*. Using the poetic form of the *Rubaiyat* itself, Jim composed a verse which he inscribed on its first leaf. The page lies before me as I write:

> *I sometimes think that never purrs so sweet*
> *The cat as when curled up at Missie's feet:*
> *Missie and Bambi in the little flat —*
> *Ah, dear old flat, it then were hard to beat!*

We found the way in which Bambi made our human interests his own very appealing. He took great interest in my hooking rugs. I would sit in a small rocking chair beside the dining room window seat and spread out my many-colored materials on it. He would lie on the soft wool and in perfect contentment watch my hook go in and out of the burlap. I made my own designs for my rugs and in the one we called the story rug (it was our own story, Jim's and mine), I wove into the design a small silhouette of a fluffy-tailed cat to represent our feline companion.

When one of Jim's classes was broadcast over the university radio, I always hooked as I sat and listened. Bambi, of course, was beside me. When the cat first heard Jim's voice come into the room, he became very much excited. He ran to the radio, looked under, over, and around it, and then returned meowing to me. I suppose it seemed to him that Jim was in that box and I ought to do something about it. I said, "It's all right," which was a phrase he understood, and he then accepted the puzzle as one of those human things that a cat need not trouble himself about.

It is when you go out of town that you feel the bondage of owning a pet. There was always the question of what to do with Bambi. If we were to be gone only two or three days, we would leave him in the apartment and Caroline Woodruff would come in every day to feed and look after him. She was devoted to him, though she considered that we spoiled him. "This is the spoiltest family I ever did see," she said to me one day, "Mr. Randall spoils you; you spoil him, and you both spoil the cat!"

Caroline told me what happened the first time we left Bambi in the apartment under her care. The morning after we departed, he met her at the door, she said, and she expected him to show her the way into the kitchen, so that she would feed him at once. Instead he led her into the bedroom. Standing on his hind legs he put his front paws on the unused bed, looked earnestly up into her face, and began to meow. He was plainly saying, "They didn't sleep here last night." She understood and assured him it was all right and that we would come back. After that he was ready to eat.

"Ain't he wise?" she often said proudly. "He knows more now than most of the university students."

For longer absences we left Bambi with Mrs. Bandy, and when she could no longer take him we imposed upon our dear friend Anna Neuber, who lived in the same apartment building as ourselves.

When one is in trouble the wordless sympathy of a pet animal is very touching. I remember well one afternoon when I was sick in bed with the flu. Jim had gone to his classes and I was alone except for Bambi, who stayed on the bed beside me but seemed uneasy. After a time he left me and went into the dining room where his toys were kept in his basket.

The next thing I knew, he was trying to put something in my hand as it lay on the coverlet. He had brought me his catnip mouse! I stroked his back but was too miserable to show any lively enthusiasm. So he decided to try again. Some minutes later he was back, offering me his rubber ball. Still I showed but little interest.

He left again. This time he went into the study where I heard him give a low cry of distress. Then there was a long pause.

He trilled to get my attention as he came back through the bedroom door. He was carrying in his mouth a sprig of pussywillow, which I knew came from the vaseful which I had put on the filing case in the study before I became ill. Flu or no flu, I had to rise to the occasion over this. I pulled myself together and praised him extravagantly. He was a wonderful cat, I told him, to think of bringing a flower to a sick lady and I was proud of him!

The occasion on which Bambi's sympathy meant the most, perhaps, was when I went to the hospital for an operation. I entered the hospital the afternoon before, so that Jim and Bambi were left alone that night. A grave apprehension was involved and Jim was terribly worried. He told me later how he sat in the fireside chair and Bambi sat on its wide arm close beside him. He could feel the cat's sharing of his troubled mood and it helped to have that quiet companionship.

When bedtime came and Jim started toward the bedroom, Bambi raised a protest. He ran to the front door and cried. His idea seemed to be that they should not go to bed because Missie had not come home yet. From all accounts the two of them spent much of that night in the fireside chair. The next morning the light came back in Jim's face at the doctor's words after the operation: "*Everything* is all right."

In the year that began the 1940's, Bambi one day showed that he was ill. We sent for the veterinarian, who was able to help him but told us the trouble was old age. Jim wrote sadly in his diary, "I was blue, very blue about this."

Bambi died two years later. Under the heading WE LOSE A DEAR PET, Jim wrote in his diary the following obituary: "Bambi has gone to where all good cats go. . . . He was very feeble & thin. Also 13 years old. Yet Polly wept and wept. He was more than just a cat. He had a personality & was like a person to us. A real companion."

11.

Work, Play, and Cherished Friendships

I now go back to our story at the point where Jim summarized the year 1938. He mentioned a sabbatical, but that semester's leave from Illinois meant too much to us to be passed over with only one word.

Though most of the sabbatical was spent in Washington, we went first to Boston to search through certain manuscripts relating to Lincoln in the libraries of the city and at Harvard. We had spent six days working side by side at this, studying old letters and papers, taking notes on them, and ordering photostats, when we had an adventure. At the end of a day's work, as we neared the Bellevue Hotel, where we were staying, a sudden wind blew my hat off. It was such a fierce wind we were very glad to get inside the hotel. Soon from our window we could see people on the street clinging to buildings to keep from being blown off their feet. Then we noticed that great trees on Boston Common were being uprooted and blown down. It was the great hurricane of September 21, 1938. As we ate dinner at the hotel that evening we heard the wild, almost human shriek of the hundred-mile-an-hour wind, a sound never to be forgotten. When we passed through the lobby after dinner, we found it crowded with men who could not get back to their homes in the suburbs.

We were ready to go on to New York for research there, but we now found we were marooned in Boston. Railroad bridges had been washed out and there was no train service. Finally, on September 26, we obtained overnight passage on a ship on the Eastern Line, according to Jim's diary. I shall never forget how beautiful the New York skyline looked in the morning sunshine as we came into the harbor. Jim had taught in the summer school at Columbia the year before and we had grown fond of New York and had many friends there. Our brief stay this time included dinner parties at the homes of such delightful people as Mr. and Mrs. Henry Steele Commager and Mr. and Mrs. Allan Nevins.

By the end of the first week in October we were settled at Washington in the happy routine of studying manuscripts in the Library of Congress. Other historians were always working there too and we never failed to have good company when we went out for lunch. At lunch we talked shop in a fine camaraderie of scholarship. Jim remarked in his diary on December 28 — Christmas vacation time — that this was the first time we had lunched alone at the Methodist Building since we came to Washington.

Both our departure from Washington (January 21, 1939) and our arrival back in Urbana were warmed by the friendships which meant so much in our lives. On the day of departure I received two corsages, and three of Jim's former graduate students, Martin Claussen with his wife Evelyn, Eugene Braderman, and Hardee Allen, saw us off at the train. Our friends the Heaton Bailys met us at the station in Urbana and flowers and invitations came in as soon as we reached our apartment.

Before leaving the 1930's, I would like to tell of one little incident which prompted a bit of Jim's humorous doggerel. The time was early morning and Jim was shaving. I brought into the bathroom the university newspaper, the *Illini*, and sat on the edge of the bathtub to read him an item which I thought interesting. The article stated that a certain patriot named William Dawes, in the time of our Revolution, rode through the countryside to give the alarm that the British were coming just as Paul Revere did. But because Henry Wadsworth Longfellow found "Dawes" a harder word to rhyme than "Revere," continued this item, William's part has been mostly overlooked.

Jim, with lathered face and razor in hand, began between strokes, to compose a poem to correct this historical injustice:

Come, my children, without a pause
And you shall hear about William Dawes.

This galloping, dashing William Dawes
Did straddle his horse in freedom's cause.

> *So down through history their names should appear,*
> *As William Dawes and Paul Revere.*

By this time I was writing down Jim's verses as they emerged. At this point he asked me if there was any rhyme for William. I said no, and I was promptly proved wrong:

> *Not Paris to the walls of Ilium*
> *Did make such haste as galloping William!*

Of course, he had to mention that William had a descendant who became Vice President of the United States:

> *With the help of various pa's and ma's,*
> *We finally came to Charlie Dawes.*

As I remember, I myself contributed the final couplet:

> *Let Paul's name be forever starred,*
> *But honor William who rode as hard.*

The 1940's came in under the shadow of war. On September 1, 1939, Jim had written in his diary: "The incredible & ghastly news is that the Germans have invaded Poland & bombed Warsaw." He was sick at heart about it. His diaries from then on contain almost daily accounts of the war which, taken together, make a sort of contemporary history of World War II. When Japan's attack on Pearl Harbor plunged our country into the conflict, Jim's agony could hardly find words.

He could not sleep that night of December 7, 1941, because of his distress.

Our sympathies went out especially to the young people we loved, the students who were in the age group which must do the fighting. Once, after we had four graduate students to dinner, he wrote in his diary: "It is more than one can endure to think of such young men becoming cannon fodder." He then quoted the question which our Caroline had asked that same week: "How did the world get so messed up?"

Jim's diaries in the 1940's seem to me especially rich in well-loved names among the graduate students. The university was by this time appointing a research assistant for him, which was quite a financial improvement over paying for such help out of his own pocket. We naturally saw more of these assistants than the other graduate students, and became very fond of them. Among the earliest appointees were Theodore L. Agnew and LeRoy H. Fischer, who would always remain two of our favorite people.

How many students did Jim have? In 1946 he was asked to submit the total number of theses he had supervised. Upon investigation he found that twenty-six Ph.D. students had written theses under his direction and fifty-five had written master's theses. These figures refer only to thesis students. The number of students in his classes, undergraduate and graduate, through the many years of his teaching up to that time, would mount up to hundreds. I cannot even mention all the graduate students in whom we took a special interest. I can speak of only a few of those to whom Jim gave acknowledgments in the prefaces of his books, and those whom he names, for special reasons, in his diaries.

Each autumn we made some special effort to get acquainted with the new graduate students. Jim's diary tells of such an occasion on October 19, 1941, when we invited four of them to have Sunday dinner with us at the University Club. The choice of meat on that day was chicken or roast lamb. There was a pause at the table while Jim was writing down the order and I was trying to help him by getting the individual preference of each guest. In that pause I sensed a certain stiffness of new acquaintance which I wanted to break up; so I turned to the serious-faced young man on my left and said with a twinkle, "Are you a chicken or a lamb?" His eyes lighted with amusement as he promptly answered: "I'm a chicken!" Aside from mere introduction, these are the first words I ever exchanged with David Donald, who would come to mean so much to Jim and myself in the future.

Early in 1940 our group of young people was increased in a most satisfactory way. Dr. Blair Harter, the husband of Jim's niece Margaret Randall Harter, was assigned as reserve medical officer at Chanute Field. This brought the young couple to live at Rantoul, Illinois, about fifteen miles north of Urbana, and we at once adopted them as our "Rantoul children." We loved the evenings when they drove down to have dinner and visit with us, especially after their little son Gregory was born. A baby in our apartment was rare entertainment.

Jim's diary for September 22, 1942, records a red-letter day. At nine o'clock in the morning the phone rang and a never-to-be-forgotten voice said, "This is Carl Sandburg." Jim had met him on several occasions and formed a cordial friendship with him and now he was stopping over in Urbana for a surprise visit.

He came over to our apartment about ten o'clock and spent the whole day with us. Jim hastily invited several friends, Rexford Newcomb, Bruce Weirick, and George Goble, to have lunch with Carl and him at the University Club. In the evening Carl had dinner just with Jim and me in our apartment.

I had not met Carl before that morning. Here is what Jim wrote about my introduction to him: "Polly felt rather timid about meeting him, but found he had a headache & cold feet, so after she had given him 2 aspirin tablets & a pair of wool socks, they were old friends." I brought out my copy of *The American Songbag* and he autographed it for "Ruth (Polly) Randall." Later, when our friendship with him had grown into a deep affection, he autographed his books to us more informally. I particularly liked his inscription in the volume *Complete Poems*, for "Jim and Ruth Randall, you fellers." I liked being a "feller."

In October of the following year Jim went to Chicago to serve on a committee with Carl and Oliver R. Barrett, the Lincoln collector, which was endorsing the plan by which the schoolchildren would help buy for Illinois a copy of the Gettysburg Address in Lincoln's own handwriting. The children could do this by giving five or ten cents apiece.

Jim spent a wonderful day in Chicago, hobnobbing with Carl, Mr. Barrett, and Ralph Newman of the Abraham Lincoln Book Shop. They talked over Lincoln matters and later Jim saw Mr. Barrett's superb collection. At the end of this day of stimulating companionship Carl invited Jim to go home with him for an impromptu visit.

Jim's diary fairly glows with enthusiasm over the interesting two days he spent with the Sandburgs at Chickaming Goat Farm near Harbert, Michigan. He was cordially welcomed by Mrs. Sandburg, whom he described as "a fine, gracious woman, full of vitality. Has a beautiful smile, so does Carl." He learned she was an outstanding authority on goats and that she was the one who managed the goat farm. Jim received quite an education about goats during his visit: he slept in the "milk tester's room," was shown the impressive herd of fine pedigreed goats, and drank his first goat's milk, which he pronounced "delicious."

The highlight of his visit, however, was the intimate association with Carl. One memorable evening the two took a long moonlight walk along the shore of Lake Michigan, a thing Carl said he liked to do at the end of the day to rest his eyes and relax. Jim recorded what they talked about in considerable detail. They exchanged opinions on many subjects: Lincoln, literary matters, politics, philosophy. They compared notes on the prolonged drudgery of writing a nonfiction biography. Carl said he wanted to write the kind of book on Lincoln that he wished he might have read in the days when he was driving a milk wagon at Galesburg. He generously praised Jim's Civil War book and his Lincoln article in the *Dictionary of American Biography*. He predicted that Jim's biography would be all the better because he had waited till that time to write it.

Carl spoke freely about people and things he disliked. But he said he did not keep his hates. This was a bit of philosophy with which Jim thoroughly agreed.

It was ten-thirty at night when Jim returned to Urbana from this trip. But it was a long time before we thought of sleep. In the way of married couples he shared with me the interesting time he had by telling me about it. The diary account includes: "Nice to be home & be with Polly after my absence. Talked at length re. the Sandburg visit."

The year 1944 was filled with significant, far-reaching events for both the Randalls. Though I was unconscious of the fact, it was for me a year of destiny. Our friendly providence, having involved Jim completely with the subject, now began to prepare the way for me also to become a Lincoln writer, something I had never dreamed of. It is easy now to trace in Jim's diaries the various factors which worked toward this end.

The first one appears on January 7, 1944, when Jim wrote in his diary: "Polly is collaborating in the prep. of the chapter of my Lincoln book on courtship & marriage. . . . She is going to write the passage (about half a chapter) concerning the married life of the Lincolns in Springfield. She is 'organized' in the dining room with card table & window seat, & is so surrounded with piles of books, notes, etc. that she 'reminds me of myself.' "

I well remember the next contributing incident. It was on the evening of St. Valentine's Day and we had the radio on. The program changed, and before we knew it we were hearing an overly sentimental, unhistoric dramatization of the Ann Rutledge legend. Believing as we did that there is no reliable evidence that Lincoln was ever in love with Ann, we listened impatiently until Jim rose and snapped off the radio. He then turned to me and told me that the papers of William H. Herndon (called the Herndon-Weik manuscripts), which had hitherto been withheld from the public, had at last become available in the Library of Congress. He added that our university had photostats of them.

Herndon, who had been Lincoln's junior law partner and biographer, was the one who had launched the Ann Rutledge legend, and these papers contained his so-called evidence. It should be possible with this full evidence to put Herndon's story of the romance on trial in the court of historical justice. Later that evening Jim wrote in his diary: "I gave the wife a new assignment . . . suggested she might go after the subject of Lincoln and Ann Rutledge."

An event of great importance to this project had taken place exactly four weeks before. David Donald, who was now Jim's graduate student and research assistant, was seeking a Ph.D. thesis subject. Jim had been wishing for a gifted student to take up the subject of Herndon, and on January 14 he suggested this to David. To remove certain "encrustations" from Lincoln biography, it was necessary that an intensive study first be made of Herndon and the value of his testimony. David accepted the subject.

So, in the months ahead, three literary projects were to be much discussed at our apartment. Jim was coming down the home stretch in writing the first two volumes of *Lincoln the President;* David, who came in every day, was working on his life of Herndon, and I, much assisted by both of them, was pursuing the subjects of the Lincoln marriage and the Ann Rutledge legend.

One can imagine Jim's disgust when in January he had to interrupt his writing to make out his income tax. The income tax form that year seemed more incomprehensible than ever, and as he read it he exploded frequently with his favorite ejaculation, "Gadzooks!" He was laboring over it one morning in his study while I, in the dining room, was trying to puzzle out the directions of a dress pattern. Not being able to make sense out of them silently, I began to read the instructions aloud. Jim, passing through the dining room and hearing me, interjected a phrase from his income tax. The effect was so comical that we both broke out laughing. Subsequently I used the incident in some light verses to which Jim gave the title "Home Economics." To my delight they were later published in the *Saturday Review.*

HOME ECONOMICS

The wife was cutting out a dress,
    And reading the directions,
She seemed to be in dire distress,
    Her pattern lay in sections.

His income tax he read and read,
    'Twas raising mental blisters,
So this is what the couple said
    (*Italics are the Mister's*).

"*Surtax net income for the year*
    Should meet small perforation,
Join skirt *and enter difference here*
    Below (*see computation*)."

"*Declare the estimated tax,*
    I think I'll pay it later;
And baste while matching center backs,
    Whichever is the greater."

"Seam A to C with matching V,
    Confound those ifs and whethers;
Take gain or loss (from Schedule D)
    And stitch, adjusting gathers."

And so their efforts they increased
    Their calculations blending.
The dress was made; for her at least
    There was a happy ending.

That spring David Donald took his preliminary examination toward his Ph.D. degree. Jim returned home from this occasion with beaming face. He wrote in his diary that night how "superior & outstanding," and "distinguished" David's performance had been. The account ended, "He certainly has the goods."

David by this time seemed like a member of the family. It had now become a regular custom to have him and several other graduate students for Sunday evening supper, at which the main dish was always scrambled eggs. David often officiated as scrambler. Jim's diary tells of the Sunday evening following the preliminary examination: "Had a bit of pleasantry, crowning David in honor of his Ph.D. The crown had the device 'Ph' — he gets the 'D' after another exam. Had a grand time." We always seemed to have a "grand" time at our "young people's parties."

In June we started on one of the most unusual vacations we had ever had. With our dear friends George and Roberta Goble we took a trip on a riverboat, the *Gordan C. Greene,* up the Ohio and Kanawha rivers. We had dropped back a century in our slow-moving method of travel as we sat on the deck and watched intimate scenes of the countryside passing by like moving pictures. We tied up at quiet little river towns which had once bustled with life in the days when the river was their great highway out into the world. We enjoyed walking across the gangplank and exploring these quaint villages. It stirred the imagination to pass them at night and see the lights of the little homes nestled on the wooded hillside.

We never tired of watching the great paddlewheel at the back of the boat as it turned round and round in the water, throwing a constant cascade of shining drops high into the air. It was all so interesting and we were kept so busy "running the boat," as we said, that we begrudged the time spent sleeping in the bunks of our tiny cabin. The purser's stock joke was that the cabins had evidently been designed by the man who wrote the Lord's Prayer on a grain of rice!

Early in July we were back in Urbana and Jim was engaged in what seemed endless revision of his Lincoln manuscript. I had finished my work on the chapter about the Lincoln marriage and on July 13 Jim wrote in his diary: "I have gone over it . . . giving it careful historical revision, yet the main work is Polly's." It was characteristic of him to be generous in bestowing credit on others. I had named the chapter "The House on Eighth Street."

His manuscript by this time had grown into a great pile on his desk, yet it took the Lincoln story only as far as the Gettysburg Address. This much was to be published the following year under the title *Lincoln the President: Springfield to Gettysburg.* The remaining half of the work was still to be written.

On November 27, 1944, Jim recorded in his diary in capital letters: "LINCOLN MS. SENT OFF." He had been working on this manuscript seven years. I had a proud sense of his achievement as I packed the precious pages, and I think he too was genuinely glad to have reached this stage in his long task. It is hard, however, for a conscientious scholar to be completely satisfied that he has done everything he should. Most authors will understand his state of mind when he wrote that day: "I have the feeling that a lot more ought yet to be done on the book. There will be quite a bit of late revision." This revision and the finishing of the Ann Rutledge analysis would be accomplished in the months to follow.

The early 1940's were good years for us. They might be called, to use Mrs. Browning's words, "sweet years, the dear and wished-for years." They had brought us precious gifts, congenial work and play, cherished friends, and deepening companionship with each other.

12.

"The Profoundest Living Student of Lincoln's Career"

On New Year's Day, 1945, Jim wrote in his diary that his scheduled events for this year included his giving the Walter Lynwood Fleming lectures at Louisiana State University and the publication of his *Lincoln the President*. On March 5 something happened which was definitely not scheduled: I had to undergo another sudden operation. Oddly enough, it took place on the same day of the month and almost the same hour as my operation four years before, when Bambi had shown such sympathy with Jim's anxiety.

I was in the hospital and under heavy sedation when Jim told me some news about his book. He said a letter had just come from his publishers, Dodd, Mead, saying they were going to bring it out in two volumes. In spite of being drugged and miserable, I was so pleased to hear this that when the doctor (our beloved Dr. Charles T. Moss, Sr.) entered to find out how I was, I insisted first on telling him about the twin volumes. I was quite ill following the surgery and Jim wore himself out coming to the hospital two or three times a day.

Living sometimes seems like riding on a roller coaster; it is a series of ups and downs. That operation was decidedly a "down" but by early May we had a definite "up." It was our visit to Baton Rouge, where Jim gave his lectures on Lincoln and the South.

In the late afternoon of a cold gray May 5, we boarded our favorite train, the Panama Limited, for the overnight journey. We were in high spirits to be going south and I remember what fun we had that evening working all the gadgets in our train bedroom. It seemed as if, by pushing a button, we could produce almost anything short of a grand piano! It was thrilling to wake up the next morning in a Southland where summer was in its full glory of sunshine and flowers. The oleanders, magnolias, mimosas, and gardenias were all in their splendid bloom. During our visit, mindful of the price of gardenia corsages in Urbana, I told our friends Alden and Vera Powell that the blossom-laden gardenia bush in their yard would be worth about five hundred dollars in Illinois. It was a special treat of our visit that the Powells were there, for Alden, then on the faculty of Louisiana State University, had been one of our favorite graduate students at Illinois.

Jim rightly described these five days in Baton Rouge as "perfect." It happened that our stay there coincided with an event which lifted the heart of the nation. Germany had surrendered and V–E Day was celebrated on May 8. The long agony of World War II was almost over. It would end with V–J Day when Japan surrendered.

The history faculty at Louisiana State University was cordiality itself. We were honored at a large reception and a number of luncheons and dinners. Jim's lectures were received with much praise. They were later published by the Louisiana State University Press in a little book entitled *Lincoln and the South*. Jim's dedication pleased me very much. I sometimes pointed out the fact that he, a Northerner or Yankee, writing on the Civil War, should have a well-balanced viewpoint since he had married a Southerner or Rebel. The dedication reads: "To the Beloved Rebel who abides with me."

Still elated with the good time we had had in Baton Rouge and carrying a box of gardenias to distribute among our friends, we returned to Urbana May 11. We were speedily brought down to earth by finding that galley proof on *Lincoln the President* had "piled up — great quantities of it," as Jim wrote in his diary, adding rather unnecessarily, "Work ahead!" We were again in the hectic stage of seeing a scholar's book through the press.

Jim's birthday, June 24, came on Sunday that year, and as usual we had several graduate students for supper, three choice ones, David Donald, Paul Hubbard, and Josephine Harper. We did not tell them it was Jim's birthday, but I did mention that he had some new pajamas. That day, in a letter to his sister Alice, he had dashed off a burlesque advertisement of these newly acquired pajamas. With his permission I read this letter aloud, to the great amusement of the young people. The line which brought down the house was: "No more safety-pinned trouser front. Why saddle infants' customs on the adult male!"

Two days later Jim wrote in his diary about a change which we were to feel keenly. David Donald, he said, "has been my incomparable assistant 2½ years." June 30 would be his last day under this appointment, though he would remain in Urbana for some weeks. I think Jim felt a little as if he had lost his right hand.

We read proof for much of the summer, and then in August came the hardest task of all, because it has to be done under the pressure of a quick deadline. Index-making, it seems to me, is the author's trial by ordeal. Jim's diary recorded "organizing an 'index factory,' giving parts of the work to various grad. students." They were paid by the hour for making out index cards. I made out index cards too, and when the cards were finished it was my job to put them in alphabetical order, all five thousand of them. Using letters from our game of anagrams I laid out the alphabet on a card table and sorted each entry under its proper letter. After I had finished, the little stacks suggested the buildings of a miniature city with the letter "S" forming one of the tallest skyscrapers. When the index was finally mailed off we felt that we "had had it."

November found us tense with expectation of the

arrival of the bound volumes. On November 12 Jim recorded how "Ruth watched eagerly for the books to come but they did not arrive." The entry for the next day breaks out into joyous exclamations: "Great excitement in the apartment! 'The books' [*Lincoln the President*] came. We are thrilled and delighted! . . . Wonderfully attractive cover design! The two vols. are nicely cased & the jacket is flattering."

Of course we both fell to a busy examination of each detail, exchanging excited comments as we did so. For Jim there was that special emotion an author has when he first sees his book in print. Publication seems to add a new dignity to one's words. I read and reread the dedication with deep feeling: "To Ruth, whose unfailing help and interest illumined the labor of these pages."

The graduate students who had done any service whatever connected with the book during the seven years of its writing were eager to look at the Acknowledgments, well knowing they would find their names there. A new name, not that of a student, appeared in connection with the index-making, that of Helen Hart Metz, a high-school teacher and expert indexer who had come into our lives as a good friend.

For the whole week following the arrival of *Lincoln the President*, we lived in a state of keyed-up excitement. The arrival was on a Tuesday. On Thursday our copy of the *Saturday Review of Literature* (as it was called then) came with a striking cover which sent me into ecstasies and almost sent Jim into shock! It was a beautiful pen drawing of Jim's face set against the profile of

Profiles

The picture on the right was on the cover of the *Saturday Review*, November 17, 1945, the issue in which *Lincoln the President: Springfield to Gettysburg* was reviewed. On the left is one of Jim's sketches of Carl Sandburg.

Abraham Lincoln, done by Frances O'Brien. Jim, with his usual modesty, felt at first that his face should not be placed beside Lincoln's. "It embarrasses me," he wrote in his diary that night. "Too much prominence. Don't deserve it." He was delighted, however, with the skill and beauty of the drawing. The original, which Frances O'Brien generously gave us later, became one of our treasures. A number of people remarked that there was a resemblance between the two profiles, perhaps spiritual as well as physical.

The next day, Friday, Carl Sandburg came to town to give a lecture at the university. Jim was in the committee which met him at the station. To our delight he had declined a big dinner in his honor before the lecture, preferring a quiet supper with us in our apartment. So we had a wonderful visit with him.

Recognizing that Jim was a bit overwhelmed with the publicity his book was getting, Carl gave him some kindly advice. Jim recorded it in his diary: "He told me not to be sensitive re. the placing of my face on cover of *Sat. Rev. of Lit.* Appropriate, he said. And he advised me to get full pleasure from my reviews while having also a thick skin for criticisms." He also gave encouragement and advice to Jim about publishing a book made up of his various Lincoln essays.

That evening Jim introduced Carl to an overflowing audience in the university auditorium. Carl's speech and his singing to his own guitar accompaniment set his listeners wild with enthusiasm. The evening ended with Carl and several of our friends coming back to our apartment to visit until midnight. That was an early hour for Carl to say goodnight. Later, more than once, we sat up with him until two and even three o'clock in the morning.

Friday, then, was Carl Sandburg day. Saturday was autographing day for Jim in Chicago, and a strenuous day it was. It included an elaborate autographing party at Ralph Newman's Abraham Lincoln Book Shop, autographing many books at Marshall Field's and at bookstores, and attending a large dinner at the University Club, where his friends had gathered to do him honor. He was pleased that Paul Angle, whom he had known as a graduate student at the University of Illinois in the year when Paul took his master's degree there, introduced him.

Jim received high words of praise for his work on Lincoln from his friends at that dinner and in the many prominent reviews that appeared in the days to follow. Almost every mail brought letters and clippings about *Lincoln the President*. As Jim wrote in his diary, they were "interesting even when they criticize." The statement which I treasured most, I think, was the one in which Allan Nevins wrote that Jim was "known to scholars throughout the land as the profoundest living student of Lincoln's career."

Our analysis of Lincoln's alleged romance at New Salem, which I had named "Sifting the Ann Rutledge Evidence," had been placed in the Appendix of Volume II. I was especially pleased when one scholarly reviewer later referred to that analysis as "completely pulverizing the Ann Rutledge myth." Our long investigation had shown there is no reliable evidence that Lincoln was ever in love with Ann.

The whole complicated process of producing a scholarly book, which we had just passed through, the long, trying preparation and the drama of its actual emergence, had been building up in my mind a comparison to another important human experience. After the excitement about the publication of *Lincoln the President* had died down, I found the idea had crystallized to the point where I just had to get it down on paper. It was the same sort of impulse which prompted both Jim and me at times to write humorous doggerel whose sole purpose was to amuse ourselves and a few close friends. So one day I sat down and wrote a little essay which I called "We Have Had a Book." After a few laughs over it with friends, I put it away with various other light scribblings of mine.

Looking back now, I think that brief skit may have played a small part in my ultimately becoming an author. To have this effect it was necessary that fate find some instrument to get it out of a folder in my files and into publication. The instrument proved to be David Donald, who had left Urbana the year before, we thought, for good. He had spent the intervening year on a traveling fellowship from the Social Science Research Council. But by now it had been arranged that he would return to the University of Illinois for a year as Jim's research associate. This would enable David to finish his biography, *Lincoln's Herndon*, before starting on his teaching career at Columbia University.

This good prospect was the background of that gala day, September 15, 1946, when David received his Ph.D. degree from Illinois. His mother had come from Goodman, Mississippi, for the event and we were enjoying her very much. I remember our lighthearted banter as we started to the campus for the ceremony. Jim and David both wore academic cap and gown and Jim, who was an excellent amateur photographer, planned to take some pictures of the newly made Dr. Donald after the occasion was over. Not wishing to carry his folding camera as he walked in the academic procession, Jim had given it to me to carry. I had managed to squeeze it into my handbag, which looked very lumpy in consequence.

David and his mother promptly became curious as to the contents of my bag. I said, "Guess." David made several ridiculous suggestions but I would not commit myself. Finally he and his mother decided it was a pistol with which to shoot the speaker if we did not like his commencement address!

David had returned to Urbana some weeks before this occasion. One day in July I had brought out "We Have Had a Book" and read it to him. He laughed over it satisfactorily, for it was meant to be humorous. Then he said seriously, "Why don't you send that to the *Saturday Review?*"

"Oh yes," I answered skeptically. "And will you pay the postage — both ways?"

David put his hand in his pocket and solemnly drew

out twelve cents (the exact amount required in those days of cheaper postage), and handed the coins to me. So, in the spirit of one taking a dare, I wrote a gay letter to the editor explaining all the circumstances about the little essay and enclosing with it a stamped return envelope. I was dumbfounded when it was accepted by return mail — and airmail at that! Jim's diary records that I mailed it on a Tuesday and received the letter of acceptance on Saturday morning.

The whole incident gave me a great thrill. I realized that the article's relation to an established work like *Lincoln the President* had been a strong factor in its favor. Nevertheless, I was proud to have something published in the *Saturday Review*. I had no plans at all for writing at this time, and if anyone had suggested that I write a book I would have thought the idea ridiculous. But I did hope I might think of some light verses or an essay to offer the *Saturday Review* later, reasoning that if a miracle like this could happen once, it might happen again!

We received our copy of the *Saturday Review* which contained my essay on the day after David took his doctor's degree. It was in the "Strictly Personal" department and it read as follows:

WE HAVE HAD A BOOK

We have had a book at our house. We use the expression advisedly. If it is correct to say, "We have had a baby," it is correct to say, "We have had a book." There is an amazing similarity between the two performances.

To take first things first, in the beginning the impend-
ing event is not revealed to the public. It is more or less a
secret known only to one's close friends and, for obvious
reasons, to publisher or physician. As time goes on, the
circle of those who know widens. The appearance of
long sheets of galley proof around the house discloses
the secret as genteelly as infants' garments used to do in
the old-fashioned movie. At this stage, for reasons best
known to oneself, one begins to decline social engage-
ments and to stay closely at home. The long, grinding
ordeal of making an index may well be called a painful
labor by those who have experienced it. And the actual
day of arrival of the offspring is one never to be for-
gotten. It is an event wrapped in tribulation and glory.

With book as with baby, one doesn't know what it
looks like until it arrives, and then it is too late to do
anything about it. The author who opens his newly
minted book to discover a misprint on the first page has
all the sensations of a parent whose baby has been born
with a birthmark on its face.

This brainchild we produced turned out to be twins.
This was not the original plan. It usually isn't. It is one
of those things announced to you by publisher or doc-
tor, those specialists in obstetric art, after an examina-
tion. It is apt to come as a great surprise.

This news came to us when the feminine half of the
partnership happened to be in the hospital and very
groggy from an operation's anesthetic and sedatives. Her
husband told her that a letter had just come from the
publishers saying that the book would be in two vol-

umes. Though things in general were rather misty, she was elated, and when the doctor entered, he was greeted with the faint but happy remark, "It's going to be twins." He looked somewhat startled, as such an event would have required considerable revision of his diagnosis. . . .

Books, like babies, resemble their parents. Both events are creative, a launching of a bit of oneself into the world and therefore associated with a sense of fulfillment. Each is a mutual interest between husband and wife, a loved topic to talk over together and plan for in quiet evenings at home. . . .

But to the public at large it is just another book or another baby in a world of books and babies. There was never a perfect specimen of either; they all have their faults. One can draw an analogy even here. Little Sue's colic is as undeniable and unexpected an error as the one on page — well, never mind what page it is on — and wee Johnny's tantrum is as embarrassing as the upside-down illustration in volume two. Both book and baby carry the family name, to add distinction to it or otherwise, and that is one of those hazards it is best not to think about when you wake up in the middle of the night.

After it is all over and the finished product has been passed upon by circles outside the family, and there have been praises and criticisms and always a thousand unforeseen complications, problems, and vexations of soul, and you remember the long painful period of effort necessary for its production, you shake your head and say: "Never again. It's too much. We are delighted to have this one; we couldn't picture life without it, but not another. We just can't go through all that again."

And then in several years, with book or baby, like as not you have to take it all back.

By the time the essay was printed, the prophecy of the last paragraph had been fulfilled. Another brainchild was on the way!

13.

Almost Looking Over Lincoln's Shoulder

The new book, which appeared the following year, was made up of Jim's Lincoln essays which had mostly already been published in various journals. Its title was taken from the final essay: *Lincoln the Liberal Statesman*. Other titles among its thoughtful articles were "The Blundering Generation" (the generation which blundered into the nation's tragic Civil War) and "The Unpopular Mr. Lincoln." The latter tells how low was Lincoln's prestige when he became President and how, in the bitter antagonisms of politics and war, he was often called such things as "Simple Susan," a "baboon," a "demon," and an "Illinois beast." The book was dedicated to Carl Sandburg, who had encouraged Jim to undertake its publication.

I would like to quote the first paragraph of the Preface, because it illustrates so perfectly the complexities of historical research. It makes one understand why a historian must try to consult every possible source and revise and check endlessly in his effort to unearth the whole of the many-sided truth:

In approaching the subject of Lincoln and the Civil War one is reminded of Saxe's poem in which six blind men of Indostan — all very learned — investigate the elephant. One by one, after feeling the side, the trunk, the tusks, and so on, each came through with his verdict. The animal was like a wall to the one who touched the side, like a spear to the one who felt the tusk. The third blind man was sure with the squirming trunk in his hands that he was dealing with a snake. The leg convinced the fourth that the creature was like a tree, the ear suggested a fan to the fifth, and the sixth, grasping the tail, knew positively that the elephant was like a rope.

The next book Jim was preparing to write was, of course, the third volume of *Lincoln the President*, which would have the subtitle *Midstream*. His diary shows that I was preparing to collaborate again on a chapter dealing with the personal life of the Lincolns. In June he wrote, "Ruth is busy with 'organizing' for her subject—the Lincolns in the White House." Nine days later he reported that I was "vigorously working" on this subject, "with emphasis on Mrs. L." Both statements indicate that providence was quietly steering me toward a subsequent undertaking of which I had no inkling at that time.

Jim could give little attention to Volume III then, for at last 1947, the year we had looked forward to for so long, had arrived. Early in January we had the first indication that the "profoundest" Lincoln student was going to be very much in demand. A telegram on the 7th asked Jim to do a Lincoln article, apropos of the opening of the Lincoln Papers, for the Lincoln's birthday issue of the *New York Times Magazine*. Our year of thrills had begun.

That spring, for two reasons, was an especially happy one for us. First, we were looking forward eagerly to this opening up of a new field of Lincoln research. The second reason is contained in a passage which Jim wrote in his diary on January 18, after he had been reading some excellent student essays: "We have a capable and serious group of students — many of them veterans." Some of them were married by this time and their young wives were an added pleasure. We had never had a better group of students or enjoyed them more.

I remember especially an occasion in May, a picnic at which some of the graduate students entertained us as their guests. Jim's list of their names brings their faces before me: Paul Hubbard with his fiancée, Henrietta, the Stanley Joneses, "including Glenna," their small daughter, the Lloyd Sorensons, "including twins," the Fred Palmers, the Ted Fisches, Maurice Baxter, and David Donald. It was a sort of farewell party, and though we were quite gay I felt an undercurrent of sadness because I knew that a number of these fine young people were ready now to scatter and go out into the world. We also knew the time was close when we must say goodbye to David, who had shared work and play with us for three and a half years. On Sunday, June 29, after David had dined with us at the University Club, Jim wrote in his diary: "His long & wonderfully efficient service with me has now terminated. How we will miss him!" The next day we left Urbana for a four-month absence to be present at the opening of the Lincoln Papers and to do subsequent research in them. The following morning our train drew into the Washington station and I felt a thrill, as always, at the sight of the Capitol dome.

After settling into an apartment at 214 Massachusetts Avenue N.E., we went on to New York, where Jim was to do some research and have a couple of conferences connected with the coming event. Two CBS men, whom he recorded as Mr. Becker and Mr. Blackwell, took us to lunch to confer with Jim about the radio broadcast for July 26. Jim, a professor fresh from his academic world, had much to learn about the elaborate details and instructions involved in putting on a national broadcast. The radio men, on their part, had to question the scholar to understand the occasion with which their broadcast was to deal. Jim's diary mentions how Mr. Blackwell "quizzed" him at length on the subject.

The next day a call came from Lester Markel of the *New York Times*. Mr. Markel told Jim he had been chasing him "all over the Middle West" by telephone, trying to get in touch with him, only to find in the end that he was right in New York at the King's Crown Hotel! An appointment was made for next day.

I thoroughly enjoyed going to the great *New York Times* building. It housed the newspaper to which, as a matter of course, we had subscribed all our married life. Mr. Markel said he wanted Jim to do a series of six articles in succession for the daily *Times* just after the Lincoln Papers were opened. Jim would not agree to this; he could not write about the papers until he had had time to study them. But he did agree to do a Lincoln article for the *New York Times Magazine* for the Sunday after the papers were opened. In the months ahead he was to write a series of articles for the magazine.

Before we left New York something happened which took me completely by surprise. Several times, in our walking about New York, we had passed a little dress shop on Fifth Avenue and I had greatly admired an embroidered dress in the window. As Jim had a masculine loathing for feminine shopping and the shop was evidently an expensive one, it never occurred to me to do anything about the matter.

I find that on Sunday, July 13, Jim had outlined in his diary his schedule for the next day. It included another appointment with Mr. Markel, a visit to his publishers, Dodd, Mead, and the last item was "In addition, I want Ruth to look in at 5th Av. & buy a dress."

He did not mention this to me and I was surprised on Monday, when we came to the shop, that he suggested we go in. A sophisticated shoplady came forward and I stood in speechless astonishment while Jim told her he wanted to order a dress for his wife just like the one in the window but with different colors in the embroidery. He carefully specified the colors he wanted, and before I knew it she was taking my measurements very minutely and the transaction was completed. It was evident that his strategy had been not to give me any chance to protest the cost! The dress had to be sent on to us at Washington. It fitted perfectly and was one of the loveliest dresses I ever had.

Jim delighted in my having nice clothes with simple lines, but "nothing frowzy," he would often say. I soon learned to have my hats and dresses sent out on approval, for his opinions were emphatic. If he did not like an article I just did not wear it!

Back we went to Washington to the gathering momentum for the great opening. By July 23 Carl Sandburg had arrived with his daughter Helga and from then on we ate many of our lunches and dinners together. A friend had placed a car with chauffeur at Carl's disposal and we had long drives with him and Helga, visiting historic places associated with Lincoln. At the National Press building Carl showed us "Newspaper Row" and introduced some of his journalistic friends.

Jim and Carl were now having long conferences in the office of the Congressional librarian, Luther Evans, about arrangements for the CBS broadcast. Jim mentions in his diary the various people connected in one way or another with that broadcast. There were the Library of Congress dignitaries, Mr. Evans, David C. Mearns, and Verner W. Clapp, and the CBS men, John Daly and

CBS Broadcast

The four Lincoln authors who gave a CBS broadcast on July 26, 1947, the day the Lincoln Papers were opened. From left to right, Jim, Jay Monaghan, Carl Sandburg, and Paul Angle. Courtesy of CBS News Photo.

Eric Sevareid. The four Lincoln scholars who were to conduct the panel discussion were, as we know, Carl Sandburg, Jay Monaghan, Paul Angle, and Jim.

And so events moved forward to that "most exciting moment," the opening of Lincoln's presidential papers at one minute after midnight on July 26, 1947. I have already tried in my first chapter to describe the stirring emotions of that occasion. That midnight opening was for Lincoln students and devotees only; the ceremony which opened the papers to the public took place on the afternoon of July 26, just after the CBS radio broadcast.

Mr. Mearns had courteously made arrangements for me to hear the broadcast in a special room of the library. Radio tends to remind one of how much personality there is in individual voices. Certainly Sandburg's beautiful rhythmic voice could have belonged to no one else. I listened proudly to Jim's voice, which had always seemed to me the ideal voice for a speaker, deep, strong, resonant, and perfectly controlled. To my prejudiced ears it was a fine broadcast.

Afterwards we attended the opening to the public, where we were interested to note in the audience Lincoln's great-grandson Robert Lincoln Beckwith and Ulysses S. Grant III. By the next day the excitement was over and most of those in that midnight crowd had departed. In the suddenly quiet Manuscripts Division we settled down to the scholar's slow, day-after-day searching through more than eighteen thousand documents consisting of nearly forty-two thousand pages. It was laborious historical research but it also held some of the thrills of a treasure hunt. There were about nine hundred items in Lincoln's own handwriting and an endless supply of the letters which poured in upon him while he was in the White House.

To read these letters from people over the country gave me a queer feeling. Physically I was in the twentieth century but mentally I was being taken back to the 1860's. The letters were the voices of individuals who were living in the agonies of the Civil War. They dealt with the present as it was then; their writers did not know that the North would win the war or that Lincoln would be assassinated. It was fascinating to look at historic events through their eyes instead of from the perspective of a later century.

Many tragic situations and occasionally an amusing one unfold in these wartime documents. I later worked up some of the small human-interest items in an article called "Little Stories from the Lincoln Papers," which was published in the *Lincoln Herald*. This article shows that Lincoln, like other Presidents, never lacked advice. He was told how to manage the war, the government, and even his own personal behavior! Here is a passage from a long letter which a cocksure gentleman wrote him early in the war: "And when you are passing lines of soldiers, reviewing them, afoot, they say you take your boys along, and straddle off as if you were cutting across lots, to get somewhere in the quickest time you can, and pay a good deal more attention to your own getting along, than to the soldiers whom you start out to review — These things dont sound well at all. . . .

Dont let people call you a goose on these *very, very,* important relations to the army. . . ."

These papers kept the state of war constantly before us. One day I came upon a telegram dated in the dark month of August 1864, and addressed to Lincoln's Postmaster General, Montgomery Blair. It read as follows: "For Gods sake entreat the President to grant a respite to the four men condemned to die tomorrow the rumor of pardon or commutation has left them wholly unprepared to die I have this moment heard that no order suspending the execution has been rec'd & all trains have left and it is said that they are to be excuted early tomorrow morning I entreat you for time for preparation for them at all events." It was signed "Charles Gwinn."

Several questions arose at once, and I quickly shared the telegram with Jim, who sat beside me. Why was it addressed to Mr. Blair instead of Lincoln? We knew that the Lincolns, in the hot summer months, moved out to Soldiers' Home and we guessed (correctly, as it proved) that the date, August 28, was a Sunday. The frantic man who sent that telegram doubtless feared that if it were sent to Lincoln at the White House, it would not come to his attention until Monday, after the grim operations of the dawn were over. Could Mr. Blair in those days before telephones or automobiles reach the President in time? Would we ever know how it all turned out?

After going through several more documents I came to a military telegram which interestingly was signed with the name of the future author of *Ben Hur*. This message shows that Mr. Blair had managed to get the first telegram into Lincoln's hands, and he had quickly sent a wire canceling the order of execution. The second telegram is addressed to "His Excellency A Lincoln Presdt U S" and it reads as follows: "I have the honor to acknowledge receipt of your despatch notifying me of the commutation of the sentence of the four men who were to be executed tomorrow & will act accordingly." It is signed "Lew Wallace Maj Genl Vols." The incident is one of many in which Lincoln interposed executive clemency to spare human lives. I whispered to Jim, "The four men were saved."

These small items were not, of course, important in the larger story. Our main purpose was to collect from the papers new historical material about Lincoln and the Civil War. We were gathering notes and photostats for Jim to use in his later volumes of *Lincoln the President*. An entry in Jim's diary shows I was also pursuing my own special interest, Mrs. Lincoln. One day he wrote: "Ruth produced quite a sensation with a big lot of volumes — about 15 — that she was studying (for letters to Mrs. L.). They were lined up on a truck next to her desk." Fifteen of the huge volumes in which the papers were processed made an impressive load for any library truck.

Anything in Lincoln's own writing was, of course, especially interesting. The papers contain a copy of his immortal First Inaugural Address with insertions and revisions in his own hand, showing how he worked over it until it reached its final form. One can imagine him pausing and painstakingly making these changes. As to the letters, we almost felt at times that we were looking over Lincoln's shoulder as he read his incoming mail.

Long hours of research are tiring, but our leisure was enriched by companionships. To our great contentment we had some of our favorite graduate students in Washington the whole time we were there. Lavern and Martha Hamand were with us until September 1 when Maurice Baxter came to take Lavern's place as Jim's research assistant. LeRoy Fischer came briefly in August and David Donald arrived on August 16 for a month's research on Herndon items.

Carl Sandburg, who had departed after the opening, also came for several weeks study in the papers. He sat near us at one of the big study tables in the Manuscripts Division and if either Jim or I found a choice item we would get up and step over to show it to him. He would do the same for us. At noon we would go out to lunch together usually with one or two of our young people added to the party, and we would all talk shop, comparing notes on what we had found in the Lincoln Papers. After lunch we would take a little walk in that interesting part of Washington, and then Carl would say, "Back to the salt mines," and we would return to work.

These lunch hours were great fun, for when Jim and Carl were together there was likely to be a lively interchange of humor. I remember one example which seemed to please Carl especially. He and Jim were lunching with Mr. Mearns that day and the conversation fell upon North Pole "firsts," meaning events which happened for the first time in a plane flying over the North Pole. Carl said perhaps some day there would be the first baby born over the North Pole. Jim answered quickly, "I suppose you would call that airborne infantry." Carl took a boyish delight in the pun.

I like to recall our wedding anniversary that summer. On August 21 Lavern and Martha Hamand and David Donald were our guests at dinner and then we spent a gay evening in our apartment. It was decided that each one would have to compose a limerick, preferably about weddings. We all knew that David (who had not yet met the lovely young woman who would become his wife) was quick to proclaim that he would never marry. So I aimed my limerick straight at him. I find that Jim wrote it down in his diary:

> *A fine institution is marriage*
> *Which David does often disparage.*
> *We hope some young miss*
> *Will remedy this,*
> *And rush him to church in a carriage!*

After all the limericks were read and laughed over, a peculiar incident happened. At one minute before nine, the exact hour at which Jim and I had started down the aisle to be married, we sat silent in commemoration. In that silence, at the precise stroke of nine, we were startled by something flying in the window on gauzy wings. It proved to be a large green praying mantis. Just how and why it had flown up to the eighth floor where there were no screens, we could not figure out. It alighted and we gathered curiously around it. We were much amused to note, by the way it swiveled its head around, that it was eyeing us with equal curiosity. "It "prayed" for us and went through other antics, so that, as Jim wrote in his diary, "We had a lot of fun with it." David carried it down in the elevator to put it outdoors again.

I gave Carl an account of our wedding anniversary when Jim was not present and he took occasion to say some things about Jim which pleased me very much. The next day I wrote to Jim's sister Alice: "Sandburg told me Jim had one of the handsomest and most beautiful faces and profiles he knew, that the profile is Lincolnian." Alice saved the letters I wrote her that memorable summer and returned them to me.

Carl left Washington on September 3. Jim saw him off at the Union Station and wrote feelingly in his diary that night: "Carl said we had had a grand visit. Gosh, how we will miss him!" He wrote back to Jim that he missed doing postgraduate Lincoln work with the two of us. That he included me made me feel I had really become one of the "fellers." It did not occur to me, until a friend recently pointed it out, that I was the only woman in the group engaged in prolonged research in the Lincoln Papers at that time.

One feature of our life in Washington came from the fact that we were near two of my sisters and their families. We had heartwarming visits to Gettysburg, where Elizabeth's husband, Henry W. A. Hanson, was president of Gettysburg College. We also went to the little town of Montross, Virginia, where we had a joyous reunion with my sister Margaret and my niece Margaret Trimble Perry and her family. There was the constant coming and going of people we were fond of. The "going" was the part we did not like, as Jim's diary shows. On September 17 he wrote that it was David Donald's last night in Washington. "Tomorrow he goes to N.Y. to begin duties at Columbia. . . . It is hard to say goodbye to David."

By this time we had given up the apartment we had sublet from a schoolteacher and had moved to a rooming house at 203 Maryland Avenue N.E. It was a house that bore signs of having been a fine residence in a former era. The curved steps that led up to the high front door had a wrought-iron railing, the ceilings were high, and our big front room on the second floor had curved glass in its bay window. We did not even have a private bathroom here, but the location was perfect for working in the Library of Congress.

Harvey Young came for research on October 1 and was able to get a room in the same house. We three had some merry breakfasts at a drugstore next door. Harvey and Maurice Baxter were nearly always with us when we went out to lunch and dinner. After dinner we really had no place to go except to our room and that presented a seating problem. The room had two comfortable chairs and one straight chair and there were four of us. I disposed of myself by piling up the pillows and sitting on the bed. The two young men saw to it that

Jim had one of the comfortable chairs and I noticed that they took turns at occupying the remaining comfortable chair and the straight one. There, in the evenings, in conversations that alternated between light and serious topics, we talked history and tried to settle all the public questions of the time. There was deep contentment back of what Jim wrote in his diary on October 16: "We all like the Wash. routine."

The time came all too soon for us to return to Urbana. Harvey and Maurice put us on our train, the Spirit of St. Louis, on the evening of October 30. After we took our seats in the Pullman section, I looked out of the window. I have a picture-clear memory of these two fine young men standing under a station light beside the tracks, making a final gesture of farewell. How much our family of graduate students meant to us!

Our arrival in Urbana was marked by the warm welcome of our friends and the sight of our Caroline's beaming face.

In November Jim received what might be called repercussions from the publicity attendant upon the opening of the Lincoln Papers. On November 25 a letter from Allan Nevins asked whether he would consider a chair at the University of Manchester, England, devoted to American thought and culture. It would continue four or five years. Again Mr. Lincoln held Jim captive in Illinois. The next day there came an invitation to speak at the "Ninth Annual Lincoln Lecture at the Cooper Union" in New York, which he declined, along with several other requests for him to speak.

One of the nicest repercussions, in my wifely opinion, was contained in David C. Mearns's two-volume work *The Lincoln Papers*, which was published some months later. Mr. Mearns referred to "Professor James G. Randall, of the University of Illinois" as "one of the most learned men ever to apply genius to the Civil War period."

As Jim wrote in his diary when it ended: "The year 1947 was a good year for us."

14.

"In You We Have Known Both"

So were the next several years. The future which we had dreamed of in our early married days, when we were living in Salem on a penny-pinching budget, had come true. Jim had become a widely known historian and many professional honors were now coming to him. We no longer had to count the pennies so carefully, though subsequent inflation makes his salary then seem very small in comparison with the salaries of today.

We were both still unduly hospitable to cold and flu germs, but Jim's physical checkup in February 1948 resulted in an excellent report. In that month his weight reached 151 pounds, which was the most he had ever weighed. He was making progress on the third volume of *Lincoln the President*.

Highlights of these years were stimulating trips for us both, sometimes to do research, often to attend historical conventions which were really reunions with old friends, and twice for Jim to do summer teaching at other universities, which led to new adventures in friendship.

These things meant much to us. I think perhaps it was the nature of both Jim and myself to give affection to our friends to an unusual degree. It was therefore a great treat to Jim to go to Chicago early in January 1948 to attend a dinner in celebration of Carl Sandburg's seventieth birthday. On his return the next day his face fairly glowed as he told me about it. Most of the Chicago Lincoln-literary group were there, he said — Ralph Newman, Preston Bradley, Otto Eisenschiml, Olive Carruthers, Paul Angle, Ben Thomas, Lloyd Lewis, Paul Douglas, Newton Farr, to mention only a few of those listed in his diary. Carl had made a speech in which he mentioned Jim's "airborne infantry" pun, and Jim had had, to his great satisfaction, several good, refreshing talks with Carl. To be in intimate communication with a rich and gifted personality gives one a lift of spirit and often a new perspective.

We felt this way again when Allan Nevins came to the University in March to give a lecture. He was our guest for lunch in our apartment and we joined Evelyn and Clarence Berdahl (who loved and admired Allan as much as we did) in giving a dinner for him at the University Club. Allan's visit was definitely a highlight for us all.

Jim received two honorary degrees that spring. Each had a special appeal, the first one taking us back to Virginia to a town not far from Salem; the second to Indianapolis and Jim's alma mater, Butler University.

It was April 10 when we started by train to Lexington, Virginia. There were three in our party, the third being Maurice Baxter, who was Jim's research assistant that year. Maurice had been deeply interested as we talked about the plans for our trip to Virginia, and apparently he longed to visit that historic old state. Finally I said, "Do you wish you were going along, Maurice?" His answer left no doubt that he did. So we took him with us as our guest and his young companionship proved well worth the cost of the journey.

At Lexington Jim and I stayed at the hospitable home of President and Mrs. Gaines on the campus of Washington and Lee. It was the house which General Robert E. Lee had lived in when he was president of the college. Of course we were taken over the whole campus with its lovely old buildings and into the little chapel where General Lee is buried. The recumbent statue of him was, as always, deeply moving. When I had first seen that statue in my young married life the custodian, who had given his usual account of General Lee to some visiting tourists, came forward to do the same for us. Seeing the emotion on Jim's face and tears on my cheeks, without saying a word he quietly withdrew.

On April 12 Jim, with seven other distinguished men, was given an honorary degree. He was the one who gave the principal address, a deeply thoughtful speech whose title was borrowed from the words of Lincoln, "We Cannot Escape History." His degree was Doctor of Letters.

His degree from Butler University was LL.D., Doctor of Laws. Going to Indianapolis at any time meant, to Jim, reunion with the two members of the original Randall family who had their homes there. (We always missed the third member, his sister Mary, who had long since moved with her household to Akron, Ohio.) Both Alice and Arthur attended the Butler commencement and proudly watched the ceremony when the degree was conferred upon Jim and the citation read. Alice, like Jim, had the gift of enthusiasm and her face was radiant. At one of the festivities we had a visit with David Silver, a former graduate student who was a favorite with us. Jim happily wrote in his diary that night that receiving this honorary degree from Butler "is a matter of real pride & satisfaction."

I always loved to visit the big-city department stores; so next morning Alice and I went shopping downtown. Jim meanwhile visited the Indiana State Library, where we were to meet him shortly before our train time. When we arrived at the library he was nowhere to be seen. We searched and waited until we grew anxious. Finally I said to the Library attendant, "Please show me where you keep your Civil War manuscripts." There we found the absentminded professor with his nose buried in the papers of George W. Julian, completely unaware of the passage of time!

Jim had accepted an offer to teach again at Columbia University that summer of 1948. We arrived on July 1 and went at once to 90 Morningside Drive, where we had sublet a lovely apartment on the third floor, high up on the steep hill which rises above Harlem. When evening came I could hardly keep away from a front window because the jeweled pattern of lights in the blackness far below was so beautiful.

We were beginning one of our happiest summers, for once more David Donald, now an instructor at Columbia, was our almost constant companion. We frequently ate lunch and dinner together, mostly at the Faculty Club. We had so many interesting things to talk about. David's book, *Lincoln's Herndon*, was in the final stages of production and the day after we arrived he was able to show us a dummy of it, a made-up book with jacket and sample pages. Jim and I had both read each chapter as it was written and had shared David's experiences in his research and writing of it, so that to me it seemed a sort of "brain grandchild." David expressed the same idea when he wrote in his Acknowledgments, "I like to consider the Randalls the 'mental godparents' of this biography."

The finished book was ready by August 12, when we were still in New York. It seemed a beautiful arrangement of providence that we should be there to share David's feelings when he first held his book in his hands. He brought us a copy right away and we had a "jubilee" over it. The dedication to the Randalls moved us deeply. Jim wrote proudly in his diary that night, "A beautiful job. We were more than thrilled with dedication & acknowledgments. Really a notable work, beautifully published." It was to prove indeed a notable book, the beginning of David's literary career. I did not know at that time its special importance to me; it would be one of the strong factors propelling me toward the writing of Mary Lincoln's biography.

What fun we had that summer "doing" New York

with David! He had lined up certain interesting and
unusual places to eat and we had various experiences
lunching or dining at them. No young college students
exploring Manhattan could have felt more lighthearted
than we did. Here is a typical entry from Jim's diary:
"With David we went down to Greenwich Village for
a little binge. Dined at 'Young China,' did some window
shopping, visited Wash. Square, walked along 'Genius
Row' (being torn down), & returned on 5th Av. bus. At
Wash. Sq. South we visited the Poetry Mart. Autograph
poems were posted for sale at 50 cents & up. One poem,
'A Valentine to the Nature of Things,' had been sold for
$1.00."

David missed one of our eating adventures which we
found amusing. Since I had never been in an automat, we
decided to lunch at one. By chance we shared a table
with a talkative, inquisitive woman who spoke with a
foreign accent. She kept asking us questions: did we live
in New York or were we on a visit, where did we stay,
why did we come to New York? Finally I told her my
husband was teaching at Columbia that summer. Greatly
impressed with meeting a professor, she exclaimed delightedly: "So soon as he spoke, I knew he vas some-
t'ing!"

New York offered numerous simple ways to have a
good time, and I don't think David and the Randalls
missed many of them. Once we went to a broadcast of
Twenty Questions, a radio program we had enjoyed in
Urbana. Twice we took a ride on the Staten Island
Ferry, paying the fare of five cents each way. On a hot

summer evening this was refreshing and we got a fine view of New York Harbor.

So much for our fun in exploring New York. On the less frivolous side we were attending lectures and meeting well-known people. General Eisenhower was president of Columbia University then and we were introduced to him at his reception for the summer faculty. Jim commented in his diary: "The General made a fine impression with his natural manner, cordiality and unfeigned friendliness."

The time came all too soon when David with Ted and Sarah Fisch saw us off on the train for home. Among the household jingles and mementos which I kept, I find a limerick by Jim which shows a conclusion we came to shortly after our return:

> *When we reached Illinois from Manhattan,*
> *After traveling on this train and that one,*
>   *And cast up accounts,*
>   *We were shy large amounts,*
> *New York makes the pocketbook flatten!*

The pocketbook would have been in better condition if it had not been for two purchases Jim made the day before we left the big city. He took me to the dress shop at the corner of Fifth Avenue and 43rd Street, the Peasant Art Importing Company, where he had ordered the embroidered dress for me the year before. This time it was a black wool suit and again he was the one who gave specific instructions for the rich embroidery. Then he saw a beautiful gold-colored summer coat, had me try it on, and bought that too!

Early in October Jim went to Chicago for another cherished visit with Carl Sandburg. The occasion was the publication of Carl's novel *Remembrance Rock*. The celebration included an afternoon party at Marshall Field's, where, as Jim's diary records, "a teeming & adoring & immense crowd" had gathered to have Carl autograph his book for them. This was followed by a large dinner of the Chicago Lincoln-literary group, which Carl entertained with talk and song. Referring back to the year before when we had been going over the Lincoln Papers and ordering photostats, he improvised a song on the theme of photostatic blues. The song drew a comical picture of Jim Randall traveling in a covered wagon full of photostats, and it was the hilarious highlight of a much-highlighted visit.

Carl's inscription in our copy of *Remembrance Rock* lies before me as I write. He autographed it for James and Ruth Randall who, he said, would need neither preface nor glossary for it.

On December 3 Jim wrote in his diary: "I worked with Ruth on her article . . . on Mary Lincoln. Read it carefully & made detailed suggestions." I called the article "Mary Lincoln: Judgment Appealed." It attempted to show, for that much-maligned lady, the need for a new trial before the court of historical justice.

Jim ended the year by attending the meeting of the American Historical Association in Washington. He had his usual enthusiastic time. But almost his final entry for

1948 is one of those brief sentences which show how he felt about getting back home: "Fine reunion with Ruth," he wrote.

The year 1949 was the one in which fate's design for me was made clear. Jim's diary records each incident or factor which led, in its latter months, to my beginning the biography of Mrs. Lincoln. During the first half of the year my intentions went no further than writing articles about her. On February 21 Jim recorded: "Ruth is working steadily on an interesting & original article."

This was also the year of Jim's retirement from teaching. It was customary for a professor's colleagues to give a retirement dinner in his honor. In March a committee of five members of the history department called at his office to issue the invitation and arrange a date. The diary reads: "I expressed appreciation, but asked that there be no dinner. I explained it was a matter of personal feeling. . . . I added that I knew they would have done it beautifully and graciously." It would have been painful to him to listen to speeches about himself; praises always embarrassed him. Some of the committee mentioned that many graduate students "would be disappointed." This was to be proved correct in June when they did something about it themselves.

Retirement inevitably has its regrets and Jim loved his teaching. But on the other hand, he was genuinely glad to have more time to complete the two remaining volumes of *Lincoln the President*.

In April we had our annual treat, the meeting of the

Some of "Our Young People"

At a history convention in 1949, former graduate students of Jim's gave an impromptu luncheon in our honor. Standing, left to right, are Paul Hubbard, Theodore Fisch, J. Harvey Young, Martha and Lavern Hamand, Maurice Baxter, John Agnew, Jeanne and Theodore Agnew, LeRoy Fischer. Seated, left to right: Henrietta Hubbard, Jim and I, Josephine Harper, Fred Palmer, Ralph Roske.

Mississippi Valley Historical Association. It was at Madison, Wisconsin, and had an unusual highlight, described by Jim as follows: "There was a special party of 'our young people' (grad. students of the U. of Ill.) at Hotel Loraine. . . . It was a graceful occasion planned in our honor." The picture taken on this occasion shows fourteen young faces around the luncheon table and it seemed like a happy family reunion.

This was an impromptu get-together, hastily arranged. Secretly the graduate students were planning their own dinner in Jim's honor which involved much thought and preparation in advance and a formidable amount of correspondence. They had decided to surprise Jim with a little book made up of four of his articles which had appeared only in periodicals, mostly the *New York Times Magazine*. Forty-one former graduate students contributed to the cost of having a number of copies of the booklet privately printed including a special deluxe copy bound in red leather for presentation to Jim. Their names appear on a front page of the book along with a moving passage addressed to "Dear Professor Randall." The passage reads in part as follows: "With mingled regret and rejoicing we have learned of your approaching retirement, after many years of teaching at the University of Illinois." The regret was not for themselves; it was explained, but for the fresh generations of graduate students "who will not know the friendly encouragement of your seminars, your thoughtful and provocative guidance in research, the warm inspiration of your personal interest. Great teachers are

few, and great men fewer. We are proud and grateful
that in you we have known both."

The rejoicing was for the fact "that a great scholar
and a great writer" would now be able to devote his full
time to productive research and writing. The four essays
had been chosen for republication "because to us they
seemed to represent the finest qualities of a great teacher
— impeccable scholarship, felicity of style, and timeliness
of subject. The title of the first essay is truly a character-
ization of your own career: 'Living with Lincoln.' "

In June we received from a graduate student a casual
invitation to dinner and Jim suspected nothing. Let his
diary tell of the occasion: "A real surprise. Some students gave us a grand dinner at the Urbana-Lincoln
Hotel. They presented a volume of my Lincoln essays,
the gift of my graduate students. . . . A most delightful and touching experience. They had been working on
it (esp. Donald, Young & Hamand) for a no. of months.
. . . After the dinner the young people were in our apt."

There was the usual publicity about Jim's retirement.
An article in *Time* had a flavor we especially liked.
Under the heading "Goodbye, Messrs. Chips" there were
comments about six well-known and favorite teachers
who were retiring that year. The passage about Jim
featured our Sunday evening suppers for students, with
scrambled eggs and good talk.

Five days after the surprise dinner we were boarding
the Panama Limited at the start of a long trip west.
Having spent the summer before on the Atlantic sea-
board, we were now headed for the coast of the Pacific,

where Jim was to teach in the summer session of the University of California at Los Angeles. Our friend Anna Neuber went with us and added greatly to our pleasure, for she too had the gift of enthusiasm. No one of the three of us had ever visited California and we were looking forward to it with great interest. We called ourselves "the forty-niners," and like the original Forty-niners, we were expecting rich adventure.

We loved our whole journey west with its stopover at the properly named Grand Canyon. I like to remember the thrill of expectation I felt as the train drew into Los Angeles. I was watching eagerly out of the window and suddenly I exclaimed, "Oh, look at that purple tree!" It was my first view of a jacaranda tree and it fittingly introduced the color and delight of our stay in California.

Everything worked out beautifully that summer. Jim enjoyed his teaching and was given an assistant to help in grading his papers, a young man in whom he became much interested. His name was Harold Hyman and he later dedicated one of his scholarly books to James G. Randall. We were graciously entertained by the head of the history department, Brainerd Dyer, by the Lincoln Fellowship of Southern California, by Justin Turner, the well-known Lincoln collector, and by other people. I wish I had space to name all the old and new friends who were so good to us that summer.

We explored California from San Diego to San Francisco. First Miss Neuber was our sightseeing companion,

and after she left, Jim's sister Alice came out to visit an
old friend in Los Angeles and joined our expeditions.
We were determined not to miss anything in that fascinating state, and to make our California experience complete we even had a small earthquake! My mind was
filled with a great big question mark one day, as I was
lounging on the davenport in our Westwood apartment,
when suddenly something gave my couch several little
pushes and the windows began to rattle.

When summer school was over we moved from
Westwood to the Athenaeum in Pasadena, to do research in the beautiful Huntington Library. And here is
where the forty-niners really struck gold and providence
gave me the final shove toward writing a biography of
Mary Lincoln.

At the Huntington Library, Norma Cuthbert, a dear
friend of ours, was soon placing before me significant
letters and manuscripts relating to Lincoln's wife. Let me
interrupt here to say, as Catherine Drinker Bowen does
in her *Adventures of a Biographer*, that I love librarians.
Norma Cuthbert was a perfect example of their enthusiastic helpfulness and resourcefulness. Some of the letters
she was showing me had been given to the library by a
relative of Mrs. Lincoln's, Commander Philip R. Baker,
who was the son of Mrs. Lincoln's grandnephew Edward Lewis Baker, Jr. Commander Baker had more
letters pertaining to Mrs. Lincoln, Norma said — and he
lived in Pasadena.

My heart leaped at this news. Of course I wanted

to see those letters. Could I meet Commander Baker? Norma, who knew him, offered to arrange for us to meet him at lunch.

One can understand how the relatives of Mrs. Lincoln were hurt at the distorted and false impression of her which generally prevailed. They had naturally grown wary of giving out any material about her, fearing it would be interpreted according to this unjust image. So it was a question whether Commander Baker, who had withheld these letters from the library, would let me use them.

Commander Baker invited us to call at his lovely home. There we met his wife and his mother, Mrs. Joseph Kittredge Choate, whose first husband had been Edward Lewis Baker, Jr., the "Dear Lewis" of Mrs. Lincoln's letters which I had been studying in the library. In the living room was a beautiful portrait of him, showing a fine and almost irresistibly lovable face. I stood before this portrait a moment and then, almost unconsciously, I said aloud, "Dear Lewis." When I turned Mrs. Choate's eyes were full of tears.

She was a wonderful lady in her eighties, and she gave me much personal information about Mrs. Lincoln in the last years of her life. And Commander Baker let us have his valuable letters photostated at the library for my use. The new material which I received during our stay in Pasadena was indeed researcher's gold. No wonder Jim wrote in his diary on August 30 how we hated "to leave the delights of this place."

Back in Urbana we settled into the routine which had

become established when I began to write articles. Jim always worked at his desk in the study at the front of the apartment. I, not having a desk, did my writing on the big round mahogany table in the dining room, placing my photostats and notes on the window seat. Our friends, viewing the setup, had long since adopted the expression that we were "living with Lincoln."

On September 19 Jim summarized my activities in his diary under the heading "Ruth's Literary Work." The September issue of the *Abraham Lincoln Quarterly* had just come out, he said, and contained my article "Mary Lincoln: Judgment Appealed." He went on to say that "some time ago" I had written, and was now reworking, an article on "Lincoln Through the Eyes of his Wife," adding that I planned to do a companion article with the focus turned around, showing Mary Lincoln through the eyes of her husband. The diary continues: "With new material recently obtained" I would "do other studies. It may some day grow into a book . . . on Mary L."

To my utter surprise I was now receiving a number of "fan" letters about my article "Mary Lincoln: Judgment Appealed." They came, as Jim's diary reports, "from Mass. to California," mostly, of course from people with a special interest in the Lincoln subject. But it was encouraging to receive them.

With so many compelling influences closing in upon me, one morning between September 19 and October 20, I faced up to the realization that I *had* to write a biography of Mrs. Lincoln. How would I begin the first chapter? I could do articles, but to organize a big, complicated, controversial subject like this was vastly more difficult. I felt the undertaking was analogous to setting out in a rowboat to cross the ocean.

I sat down at the dining room table and haltingly wrote a few sentences. Mentally groping my way, writing and crossing out and rewriting, I shaped up a tentative first chapter. I was to continue this uncertain, trial-and-error progress until I had four or five tentative chapters. By this time Mary Lincoln had come alive to me and I felt that I *must* go on with her story as a matter of historical justice.

I had reached the feeling (which I have had ever since when writing) that I was telling the story to an imaginary person beside me, a nice intelligent person, a good listener. I must tell it accurately and simply, so that this invisible person would understand it clearly. On October 20 Jim wrote in his diary: "Ruth is working steadily each day, shaping up her book on *Mary Todd Lincoln*."

Yes, we had been "living with Lincoln." Now Mrs. Lincoln had definitely moved in with us!

15.

"The Precious Life-Blood of a Master-Spirit"

Mrs. Lincoln had not only moved in; she was taking up a good deal of the time of her husband's biographer. Jim's diaries show that, along with his own writing, he was giving constant attention to mine, reading each chapter as I wrote it and making suggestions. They were usually safeguarding suggestions. He was careful not to change my way of writing or my rhythm and organization. Along with his comments were always words of encouragement or praise.

I did not know that every few days he put in his diary a passage telling of my progress. Here are typical examples: "Ruth is tooling along beautifully on her book on Mrs. Lincoln." "She writes & studies with great enthusiasm. It will be a fine job." His diaries show deep interest and unmistakable pride in what I was doing.

In the fall of 1949 we had the privilege of visiting with some very special people. Early in October we rode to Springfield on what might be called an anachronism, an ancient interurban. The occasion was the fiftieth anniversary of the Illinois State Historical Society, of which Jim was a director. For several glorified days we hobnobbed with those rare friends Carl Sandburg and Allan Nevins.

We fell back at once into the old companionship with Carl and walked the historic streets of Springfield with him as we had walked those of Washington. I remember one day he was reluctantly debating whether to get a haircut. He asked our opinion hoping, I think, that we would talk him out of it! This we sincerely did. We liked the shagginess of his pure white hair, especially the one unruly lock which always fell down on his forehead.

One of the brightest highlights of our Springfield visit was a dinner given by Governor Adlai Stevenson at the stately Governor's Mansion. In seating his guests the Governor placed me at his right hand. It seemed that my recently published article "Mary Lincoln: Judgment Appealed" had been read by many who were attending this meeting, the Governor among them, and he devoted quite a bit of time to asking me questions about Lincoln's wife. It was a very stimulating evening we spent at the Governor's Mansion. In fact, the whole week in Springfield was refreshing, interesting, and full of the satisfaction of being with people we greatly enjoyed. Jim's diary mentions Irving Dilliard, the Jay Monaghans, David Felts, the Ben Thomases, the Roy Baslers and a number of others.

On February 12, 1950, the article which I had called "Lincoln Looks at His Wife" appeared in the *New York*

Times Magazine. The editor had changed the title to 'Mrs. Lincoln Revealed in a New Light." I had had quite a bit of correspondence with the editor, who had proved so friendly and helpful that I sent him also the companion article, "Mrs. Lincoln Looks at Her Husband." He wrote back that they could use only one article for the Lincoln's birthday issue but he suggested that I might save it and resubmit it for the next year. This I did and it was published then under the title "Mr. Lincoln: A Portrait by His Wife." I was greatly thrilled to see something I had written published in the *New York Times.*

Book-writing went on steadily in study and dining room. On January 28, 1950 Jim recorded in his diary that I had about "6 chapters in rough draft." Mr. and Mrs. Lincoln were keeping us busy and giving us many things to talk over. Frank Freidel, then a member of the history department at the University of Illinois, was often a welcome member of our literary consultations. He was writing his biography of Franklin D. Roosevelt and had many problems similar to ours. Our apartment lay on his way home from the campus, and he frequently dropped in and sometimes had impromptu lunch with us along with stimulating shop talk.

Frank and I were both in the stage when we were considering to what publisher we would first offer our manuscripts. In anticipation of this problem, I had, at one of the history conventions, conducted my own private poll on publishers. Many of our friends at the meeting had published historical and biographical books and I asked about their experiences with various publishing houses. I collected a great deal of interesting material, some of it highly emotional, but one firm stood out with a high, clear rating: Little, Brown and Company of Boston. In the end both Frank and I signed up with Little, Brown, he first. I think we influenced each other in this decision.

That spring Carl Sandburg came again to Urbana to give a lecture. He stayed with Bruce Weirick, an interesting bachelor professor of English, and we spent the evening of his arrival at Bruce's home. The "evening" included the early morning hours too, for we could not break away until after 3 A.M. This was a common experience in spending the "evening" with Carl.

Carl read to us the preface to his forthcoming *Complete Poems*. According to Jim's diary, it was "all about what poetry is." Bruce disagreed with this choice of subject and said a preface should tell about the author, "who & what he is, how he felt, his inner thoughts, how he came to write what he did." Carl said this would take too many thousands of words. The argument became spirited, and in the midst of it, Carl, perhaps noting the lively interest in my face, made the side remark to Jim that Ruth was "enjoying the fight." So were the two combatants!

Jim further wrote in his diary that the talk ran on "all kinds of topics." Carl gave an amusing takeoff on the poet Browning, and made various comments on Robert Frost, Archibald MacLeish, and other friends of his. When asked why Lincoln chose a man like Herndon for his junior law partner, Carl said one reason was that he could relax with Herndon, put his feet up on the table. I think Carl enjoyed the companionship of that evening for the same reason: he could relax. In his lecture next day to an overflowing audience, when he talked and sang, he dedicated one song to Bruce Weirick and Jim and Ruth Randall, adding some gracious words about our helping him.

During his visit Carl, along with Bruce, had home dinner in our apartment one evening. Of course I told him about my biography of Mrs. Lincoln. This was the occasion on which he gave me the advice "Write it in your own way and write it as a woman." He added further remarks which were equivalent to saying "and don't let anybody try to stop you!"

My research required going to Fort Wayne, Indiana, to Chicago, to Lexington, Kentucky, and to Springfield, Illinois. Formerly I had gone on Jim's research expeditions to help him; now he went on mine to help me. Everywhere we received the most cordial cooperation. The staffs of the Lincoln National Life Foundation, the Chicago Historical Society, the Illinois State Historical Library, and the Abraham Lincoln Association laid their treasures of manuscripts before us. The Abraham Lincoln Association at Springfield (of which Jim was a director and member of the editorial board), was then preparing a much-needed full and correct edition of Lincoln's writings. Jim was the one who suggested the name *The Collected Works of Abraham Lincoln* for the eight volumes (plus an index volume) which ultimately appeared in 1953.

We had wonderfully good times on these scouting expeditions where we met such interesting and obliging people. Perhaps the happiest of all our research trips was the one to Mary Todd Lincoln's girlhood home, Lexington, Kentucky. We went in the month of May when that lovely historic town in bluegrass Kentucky was at the height of its beauty and charm. I remember how, when we arrived, I sniffed eagerly at the soft Southern air, so like that of Virginia.

During our several days there, we were in the hands of two Southern gentlemen we knew, Mr. William H. Townsend and "Squire" J. Winston Coleman. Mr. Townsend was the author of *Lincoln and His Wife's Home Town*, one of my favorite books, which I knew almost by heart. The Squire was well known for his writings on Kentucky history. The interest and generous hospitality of these two made our visit one of pure delight. They took us to all the historic places connected with Lincoln and the Todd family and told us so much intimate detail about them that soon we felt we were living in the very atmosphere of Lexington as it was in young Mary Todd's day. This is a feeling which means a great deal in writing biography. Mr. Townsend had a fine private collection of manuscripts pertaining to Mary Lincoln and the Todd family and was generosity itself in letting me use them. It was another case where a safe-deposit box was opened up to let me have access to precious letters and documents.

That summer of 1950 brought deep sorrow to Jim and me. In the space of one week my sister Margaret was killed in an automobile accident and Jim's brother Arthur died of cancer. Both were wonderful individuals whom we especially loved and it was very hard to give them up. Jim wrote in his diary: "Ruth's grief for her sister Margaret matches mine for my brother."

By the time New Year's Day had ushered in 1951 Jim had received one of the highest honors which can come to a scholar in American history. He had been elected vice-president of the American Historical Association, which meant that the following year he would be elected its president. His diary shows that he felt humble rather than proud of this honor, but there was nothing humble in my wifely enjoyment of it!

During this year the dual literary efforts in our study and dining room continued. On July 12, 1951, Jim wrote in his diary, "My Vol. III is, in a way, nearly finished." It had been the original plan that I would write a chapter on the Lincolns in the White House for him, but this was before I became involved in writing Mary Lincoln's biography. Jim felt, under the changed circumstances, that he had better write this chapter himself, using my material. On September 1 he wrote in his diary: "Started in on some recasting for Vol. 3. Decided to give more attention in this vol. to Mrs. Lincoln, and to introduce a new chapter, 'Lonely White House Pair,' including new material along with parts of what I now have in Chap. 1: 'Presidential Days.'"

I remember how that day he silently walked from his study into the dining room, where I was working, and laid a note on my table. That note lies before me as I

write and it shows, I think, something of the joy and fun
we had in working together. It reads as follows: "Memo
for Chief of Staff. Private Randall reporting – I have
already written up social affairs in W. House & death of
Willie. Subject to rewriting and shifting. We had better
consult. JGR."

The consultation took place at once and was evidently
productive, for on September 9 I wrapped up the manuscript of Volume III, *Lincoln the President: Midstream*,
and it was sent off to Dodd, Mead. My labors also bore
fruit before the year ended. On December 27 I sent the
first twenty-nine chapters of *Mary Lincoln: Biography
of a Marriage* to Ned Bradford of Little, Brown and
Company in Boston. He had written me expressing a
wish to see the manuscript and, knowing how long it
often takes a publisher to reach a decision about a book,
I thought I could possibly write the remaining five chapters before a verdict was reached.

On January 1, 1952, Jim, as usual, summed up the
prospects for the New Year: his Volume III would go to
press, which would involve proofreading and index-
making, he must write his presidential address for the
American Historical Association and start work on Volume IV, and I would be finishing my biography of Mrs.
Lincoln. Never had our life together been richer or more
full of interest. Yet this was the year in which we would
learn that Jim's days were numbered.

For the first four months we had no inkling of his

impending illness. His annual medical checkup the summer before had revealed only a slowly functioning gall bladder, and Dr. Charles T. Moss, Jr., who had become our doctor when his father's health failed, had put him on a fat-free diet. We attributed his loss of weight to this diet.

So there was no apprehension to mar our excitement and pleasure when, on January 25, I received a telegram from Ned Bradford of Little, Brown. I had not known exactly what to expect about my book but I anticipated having to make several attempts to find a publisher. I knew only too well that scholarly books (unless they were textbooks) were not as a rule profitable financially to either publisher or author. (A professor profited indirectly from the prestige of a scholarly work, but I was not a professor.) My biography on such a controversial subject as Mrs. Lincoln had to have footnotes giving documentary proof of my assertions. Its scholarly paraphernalia of bibliography and footnotes would greatly increase the cost of publication. I realized that Jim's reputation as a Lincoln scholar was one of my greatest assets, and several other publishers had asked to see the manuscript, but I did not expect the problem of publication to be an easy one.

Consequently I could hardly believe my ears when Mr. Bradford's wire was read to me over the phone. The original telegram lies before me as I write; Jim also delightedly copied it in his diary. It reads: "Your manuscript significant contribution to Lincoln scholarship.

Charmingly written and altogether satisfying. Congratu-
lations on a very real accomplishment. Need I add all
here exceedingly eager to publish. Letter follows."

What a red-letter day that was for us and how my
spirits soared! A party at the Freidels' was scheduled for
that evening, a party that included besides the Freidels
other close friends of ours, Fay and Charlie Nowell and
Rose and Dick Current. It was a celebration of the
telegram. I remember Dick Current saying he did not
know publishers *ever* sent telegrams like that! All four
of the men present were experienced authors and how
we did talk shop!

Little, Brown at once offered me a contract. I knew
they were the publishers I wanted, but one thing
troubled me. My book was a long one and I knew of a
number of cases where publishers asked authors to
shorten their works. I felt that I could not cut my
manuscript on Mary Lincoln without weakening it. So I
suggested in my answering letter to Mr. Bradford that
we delay the signing of the contract until we had talked
further about the publication.

Mr. Bradford came to Urbana on April 1. We were to
meet him at the Urbana-Lincoln Hotel that evening for
dinner. I shall never forget the excitement I felt as we
went to the hotel. It was like the thrill I had had at
Christmas when I was a child who still believed in Santa
Claus and fairy tales. It seemed to me like a fairy tale that
I was going to have a book of my own, the book I had
worked on so long.

Jim and I had most satisfactory conferences with Mr. Bradford that evening and the next day when he came for lunch in our apartment. By the time he left I had asked him if he thought the book was too long and he said he did not, and I was ready to sign the contract. It was the beginning of a long and happy relationship between author and editor in which I would constantly and confidently turn to him for guidance.

In Jim's diary for the rest of April and early in May, I find revealing comments about his feeling "weary & under the weather." On April 28 we started to Austin, Texas, where he was scheduled to give a lecture. My brother (whom I still called "Boy," much to the surprise of his children) was at that time president of the University of Texas. We of course stayed with him and his family. We were elaborately entertained and many lovely things were done for us, but my memory of that visit is shadowed by a great anxiety. It was on that trip I realized how weak and pale Jim had become, and I had a dark foreboding that he was seriously ill.

On our return Dr. Moss put Jim through a number of tests. Finding that his red blood count was very low, the doctor ordered three blood transfusions in as many days. This resulted in a great improvement.

The improvement, however, did not hold up. Blood counts, tests, transfusions, and medication continued with ups and downs until July, when Dr. Moss arranged for Jim to be examined by a blood specialist at the University of Illinois research hospital in Chicago. Our friend Anna Neuber and I made the trip to Chicago with him and saw him settled in a room at the hospital before we returned to Urbana.

The next morning I was surprised when Dr. Moss came unannounced to our apartment. He told me he had received by phone the report on the tests in Chicago. His distressed face showed me that it was terrible news. A sample of Jim's bone marrow had revealed that he had leukemia. I was stunned. I knew just enough about the disease to say, "Leukemia? Cancer of the blood?" Dr. Moss went on to tell me gently that there was no cure for leukemia. He added that sometimes there were remissions in which the disease became inactive. Also, people with leukemia had been known to live for a long time. He was giving me this faint hope to cling to. When Anna and I brought Jim home, Dr. Moss told him the truth about his illness.

During the seven months that followed, never once did Jim complain or put into words what this death sentence meant to him, to face the fact that he must leave all that he so dearly loved, our life together, all his friends, and his work. He wanted passionately to finish his greatest achievement, the four-volume *Lincoln the President*. The fourth and last volume was about half written and he so hoped that he could win the race against time and complete it. He knew that if he gave way to his sorrow, it would make things harder for me. I, too, kept my feelings under rigid control, knowing he could not endure to see my tears.

The doctor was able, with blood transfusions and

certain drugs, to bring about periods when Jim felt much better physically. On August 8 he wrote, "I feel fine." Each time this happened we grasped at the hope that a remission was starting. But soon the red blood count dropped again and the building-up had to be repeated. Charlie Nowell spread the word that transfusions were needed and he and many other dear friends donated their blood.

Knowing that he could not get well, Jim quietly arranged that we do certain difficult tasks together, so that later I would not have to do them alone. In August we conferred with our attorney, Mr. J. G. Thomas, about bringing our duplicate wills up to date. It was silently understood that Mr. Thomas would be my legal adviser later. Then one day Jim and I went out to the cemetery just south of the campus, and selected a small lot. It was the same pleasant cemetery in which we had loved to walk in our early days in Urbana when we were young.

We were trying now to make our days as normal and cheerful as possible. We had that frail hope that Jim still had a long time to live. Except for more rest periods he was going on as usual and writing on Volume IV. It was fortunate that we were both doing work which demanded close concentration. With my biography of Mrs. Lincoln now finished and in production at Little, Brown, I had started a book which was ultimately published under the title *The Courtship of Mr. Lincoln*. As I was to explain in its foreword, in my large biography I had to present the romance of Abraham Lincoln and

Mary Todd in an unfitting atmosphere of argument and refutation of distorted ideas about it. In this little book I wanted to tell this great American love story as historical evidence shows it, with all its dramatic elements — broken engagement, family opposition, secret meetings of the lovers, and a challenge to a duel — without stopping to argue.

Our friends came to see us and we accepted invitations to dinner. Seeing how Jim's face lighted up in the presence of persons who had his affection, I would sometimes ask three or four friends to come in on Sunday afternoon for a cup of tea. We seemed to be going along on the thin surface of things while under that surface lurked the dark knowledge of his fatal illness. Often in unguarded moments there would be a sharp breakthrough of realization.

Once, after we had received a tornado warning over the radio and I was standing at a window watching the ominous sky, I thought how kind it would be if fate would have that deadly menace come our way and let us die together. And frequently at night when I finally relaxed into a doze, my body would jerk awake with the awful knowledge that Jim was doomed. I knew he too had these despairing moments.

On September 23 his Volume III, *Lincoln the President: Midstream,* arrived. His diary commented briefly on its production: "It is a fine job." Its dedication read: "To Ruth Painter Randall, biographer of Mrs. Lincoln." The dedication of my forthcoming *Mary Lincoln* would say simply, "For Jim." In my then unknown future there would be further and more specific dedications to him, so that, as Ralph Newman once said, the story of our marriage is written in our dedications to each other.

Six days later the galley proof on my *Mary Lincoln* arrived. Jim took time from his own writing to read it. His presidential address for the American Historical Association was now completed and he had set his heart on going to the Washington meeting to deliver it.

But by December the inexorable disease was closing in upon him. He had grown increasingly weak, pale, and thin. When my hand lay in his, I noticed how gray his skin looked against the normal flesh tones of mine. On the day before Christmas Dr. Moss was forced to forbid the trip and Jim arranged for Professor Arthur Bestor to read his address for him. It was a bitter disappointment to him to miss this high moment of his career.

On Christmas morning that valiant little person Jim's sister Alice came from Indianapolis bringing half a roasted turkey for our Christmas dinner. Jim recorded in his diary how much it meant to us to have her.

In January 1953, he received a letter which brought him both pleasure and sharp regret. It was from Harold W. Dodds, the president of Princeton University, saying that the trustees wished to confer the honorary degree of Doctor of Letters upon him in June. Mr. Dodds was an old friend from the year before our marriage when Jim was at the University of Pennsylvania. They had been part of a group of young men who frequently went places and ate together. Jim had to reply that in his present state of health he could not promise to come to Princeton in June.

On January 12 Jim wrote in his diary: *"Ruth's book. The book, Mary Lincoln, arrived, giving us a great thrill. It is beautifully published."* He continued at length with other delighted comments. I had never seen him show as much pleasure as this over the arrival of his own books.

I had long been scheduled to go to Chicago on Saturday, February 7, for autographing, and elaborate preparations had been made. Jim was in one of his built-up periods and Alice returned to be with him while I was away. My publishers were launching *Mary Lincoln: Biography of a Marriage* with a great deal of publicity. They gave a huge luncheon that Saturday with reviewers and many other people prominent in the literary world as their guests. There was an autographing party at the Abraham Lincoln Book Shop that afternoon, and then courtesy required that I stay over in Chicago to autograph at all the leading bookstores. My editor, Ned Bradford, came from Boston for the occasion, and he and E. Richmond Gray, of the Chicago office of Little, Brown, extended every thoughtful courtesy. I had asked my dear and understanding friend Fay Nowell to go with me, for under all the circumstances it was not easy for me to play the part required. I kept in touch with Jim by telephone.

That Sunday Jim and Alice had an exciting time reading the reviews of *Mary Lincoln* in all the papers and listening to some radio publicity. I came home Monday evening. Jim, who had spent the day in robe and slippers, dressed in his best suit for my coming. The sight of his pale, thin face lighted with joy and pride as I told my adventures is one of my most poignant memories. Five days later he hunted up a pretty card and wrote on it: "To My Valentine, The lovely — and now most famous — Ruth Painter Randall. Am I *proud* of you! Love, Jim."

One day around this time he quietly outlined to me what I must do after he was gone. He knew now he could not finish his fourth volume, and I was to ask Dick Current to complete it from his notes and material. He told me not to give up to my grieving but go on living normally and resume my social activities with my friends. *"Keep on writing,"* he continued, and I thought despairingly to myself, "How can I go on writing without you?" With his usual selflessness he said, "It hurts me to know how you will be hurt."

The last entry in Jim's diary was written on Tuesday, February 17. Carl Sandburg was in town and came to see us. Jim's face lighted up with pleasure and affection as the two talked together. Carl praised *Midstream*, saying it was a "lovable" book. Almost the last words in the diary are: "He [Carl] looks well. . . . Kissed Ruth on leaving and took both my hands."

On Wednesday evening Jim collapsed. Dr. Moss called an ambulance to take him to the hospital and then gently told me that I had better phone Jim's sister Alice to come back at once. She took the first train next morning. On Thursday and Friday Jim was conscious only at intervals. Once as I stood by his bed, he roused, kissed my hand, and said, "Sweetheart." He died Friday night about eleven o'clock.

Our friends rallied round doing everything in their power to help. My brother and my sister Julia came to sit with me at the funeral. Our minister, Dr. Joseph R. Laughlin, was deeply understanding. As he and I planned the simple services together, I gave him a quotation which I thought appropriate to use in speaking of Jim's work and achievement. The quotation is from John Milton: "A good book is the precious life-blood of a master-spirit, embalmed and treasured up on purpose to a life beyond life."

Jim was buried in Mount Hope Cemetery in the lot for two which we had selected together the summer before.

16.

"Keep On Writing"

Numbly I began to take stock of what my changed existence meant. In some cases it even involved using different terms; I was no longer a wife but a widow. I remember how hard it was for me to stop saying "our apartment." It was only my apartment now but it hurt each time I said "my" because I felt as if I were shutting Jim out.

I was confronted with many problems new to me. The greatest of these was my financial insecurity. Jim and I had saved and invested a moderate amount of money but the income from it did not bring in nearly enough for me to live on. Inflation had lowered its value and this was true also of the limited insurance he had carried. A most unfortunate circumstance was that Jim had been under the former retirement system of the university, which unlike the present system gave no consideration to the widows of its professors, and his pension ceased on the day of his death. The royalties on his scholarly Lincoln books were quick to dwindle. His Civil War textbook did better but it needed to be revised and brought up to date on recent scholarship.

In sleepless nights my mind went round and round over the question of what I should do. If I rented my bedroom and slept on the davenport in the study, that would help with the rent. I knew my brother and three remaining sisters would be willing to help me if I were in need but that thought was intolerable to me.

Mr. Thomas, who had drawn up our wills, went over my financial situation with me. I could not possibly have had a wiser or more understanding counselor. He took a warm personal interest in my problems and it was a great comfort to have his guidance. One thing he did at once; he had me take out a Social Security card, in case the royalties from my book qualified me for Social Security.

Providence had resumed its role of pointing out the way to me. The things that were now happening to *Mary Lincoln: Biography of a Marriage* were incredible to my mind. It was getting splendid reviews and I could hardly believe my eyes when I saw it in the best-seller list of the *New York Times*, where it remained for quite a number of weeks.

Another great surprise was getting dozens upon dozens of fan letters. They came from all kinds of people, from a member of the Supreme Court of the United States to a sensitive teen-age Canadian girl, hopelessly ill in a hospital, who had found joy and forgetfulness for a little while in living in the bygone world of the Lincolns. These letters indicated a widespread sale. Mr. Bradford, possibly realizing that I had given little thought to any financial return from the book, had said

to me at the autographing party in Chicago that I was going to make some money. As I remember, I answered that that would help with our doctors' bills. I did not comprehend the success which he expected for the book.

I decided that if I could make money, even a little, by writing, I would try to do it. It might furnish the supplement to my inadequate income which I so badly needed. I dreaded trying to go on without Jim's guidance, but he himself had said to me: *"Keep on writing."*

I had finished several chapters of *The Courtship of Mr. Lincoln* before Jim's death. He had read these chapters and I knew he wanted me to complete the work. The necessity of concentrating on this writing was a help to me at this time. I could momentarily forget my present distress in going, in imagination, into that quaint little prairie town of Springfield, Illinois, as it was in the first half of the nineteenth century and piecing out in detail the romance of two very interesting young people. To get the material for my "piecing" I had the rare treasure of letters written by Abraham Lincoln and Mary Todd themselves in the days of their young manhood and womanhood. I also had letters of their close and informative friends.

So I went on working on *The Courtship* as much as I could at this time of many demanding tasks. My mail was overwhelming; the flood of fan letters was equaled by many, many letters of sympathy. They came from all over, these letters of appreciation and praise of Jim's work and of outstanding affection for him. I shall quote one such letter. Wayne Temple, who had been Jim's

research assistant for the last several years of his life, wrote my sister-in-law, Alice: "Dr. Randall was the kindest man whom I've ever known. . . . He knew everyone . . . and they all loved him."

One of my first obligations was to act as Jim's literary executor. Brainchildren, like other offspring, have to be looked after. Jim had left his fourth volume, *Lincoln the President: Last Full Measure*, about half finished and he had told me to ask his colleague Professor Richard N. Current to complete it. Dick readily agreed and that difficult problem was solved in an unusually happy way. I felt sure of what later proved to be true, that Dick, using Jim's notes, would do a beautiful job with it.

Jim's books were soon to show that they indeed had "a life beyond life." About three months after his death I received a momentous letter. It told me of the announcement by Columbia University that J. G. Randall's *Midstream* had been awarded the Loubat Prize of one thousand dollars "for the best work printed and published in the English language on the history, geography, archaeology, ethnology, philology, or numismatics of North America during the five-year period ending January 1, 1953."

The news brought pride, gratitude, and pain. It seemed as if that thousand dollars was a present from Jim at a time when I was worried about money. But how it hurt that he could not know about it and that we could not rejoice over it together.

I finally completed *The Courtship of Mr. Lincoln* and sent the manuscript to Ned Bradford. It meant every-

thing to me that I had an established relationship with a leading publishing firm and a most considerate editor. He accepted the manuscript of *The Courtship* with seeming satisfaction but presented a reason for delaying its publication. The editors of Little, Brown thought the logical book to follow my *Mary Lincoln* should be one about Lincoln's sons. Mr. Bradford outlined the plan for such a book and offered me a contract for it.

I was delighted with the idea and the challenge of it, though I did not sign the contract at that time. Since I try to write only authentic biography and never fictionalize, I have to be sure I can get adequate research material for a book before I bind myself to write it. I asked for time to do research, mostly on Robert Lincoln, before signing.

Then I settled down to the same earnest research I had used in writing Mrs. Lincoln's biography. And here I had an experience that was to be repeated several times: an incident occurred that gave me the feeling that Jim was still guiding me. Among his papers I found a file on Robert Lincoln that he had kept through the years of his Lincoln research. It was a great help and it gave me an uplift.

Again, as in the study of Mrs. Lincoln, I had cordial assistance from librarians and others who had to do with historical material. A wonderful friend in Lexington, Kentucky, Mr. William H. Townsend, courteously gave me the use of more than fifty family letters written by Robert Lincoln, new and revealing letters. The long list of those who assisted me in my writing of *Lincoln's Sons*

appears in its Acknowledgments. I soon discovered I had adequate material for the book Little, Brown had suggested and I then signed the contract.

Lincoln's Sons was published in 1955. Its dedication is to those best-loved individuals in my life to whom I owed the fact that I had become a writer. It reads: "To these two: F. V. N. Painter who was my father, and J. G. Randall who was my husband."

Meanwhile, many exciting things were happening to the biography of Mary Lincoln. It had been adopted by the Atlantic Monthly Book Club, Doubleday's Family Reading Club, the Christian Herald Family Bookshelf, and had been made available through the Literary Guild. It was condensed by the *Reader's Digest* in their July 1953 issue and was selected for ten of their international editions.

At Christmas the *Reader's Digest* graciously sent me copies of these foreign editions which contained the condensation in various languages. I was intrigued to see my book under such titles as *Mary Lincoln: Biografia de um Casamento* (Portuguese), *Abraham Lincolns Frau* (German), *Storia di un Matrimonio Famoso* (Italian), and *Maria Lincoln: Biografía de un Matrimonio* (Spanish). The last-named brought me a fan letter from a courtly Spanish gentleman who signed himself with a proper conventional phrase which when literally translated meant "Your most affectionate admirer!"

I especially liked the Japanese edition, in which the first pages began at the back and my name was the last thing in it at the front! With the help of friends I soon

had all the languages identified except the one in which the title was *Mary Lincoln — Suuren Presidentin Puoliso*. It was a week or so before someone dropped in who was able to tell me that was the Finnish edition.

Mary Lincoln continued to give me thrilling surprises. In January of the following year the American Library Association listed it as one of "the most notable books of 1953." Before long it was put on talking records for the blind and later I had a letter from the person who had spent months putting it into braille.

Lincoln's Sons also was put on talking records and was distributed by Doubleday's Family Reading Club. A long condensation of it, featuring Tad Lincoln, appeared in *McCall's* magazine for January 1956. That same year I had again the warm feeling that Jim was giving me a present of a thousand dollars. His fourth volume of *Lincoln the President*, which had been completed by Professor Current, was awarded the Bancroft Prize of two thousand dollars by Columbia University. The award was divided equally between Professor Current and me. I like to think that this award also implied a tribute to the whole four-volume work to which Jim had given so much of his life.

I flew to New York to attend a banquet at which the award was presented. It was on this trip that I had the joy of meeting and giving my full affection to David Donald's wife, Aïda, a lovely woman who is a scholar in her own right. When, a couple of years later, the Donalds were expecting a baby, they agreed that, boy or girl, this offspring should have "Randall" as one of its names. Thereby hangs a tale. David, at my request, was revising Jim's *Civil War and Reconstruction*. So it came about that the revised edition, bearing the names of both authors, had a dedication which also combined the two names; it read: "For Bruce Randall Donald." What a lot of personal history there is in dedications!

Little, Brown brought out *The Courtship of Mr. Lincoln* in February 1957. It was reprinted in full in *Best-in-Books* next to excerpts from John F. Kennedy's *Profiles in Courage*. The dedication of *The Courtship* reads: "For Jim who read the early chapters of this book — and asked me to finish it."

Its publication was almost exactly four years after Jim's death. My books had sold well and they had shown me a way to help support myself, for which I shall always be grateful to a kind providence. One day I asked Mr. Thomas if he thought I could afford a trip to England. He answered that he thought that was a fine idea. So, on April 24, with my sister Laura and a friend of hers, I boarded that good ship the *Queen Mary*.

I kept a day-by-day journal of that expedition abroad which would make a little book in itself. It is sufficient here to say I loved everything about England and Scotland except the climate. I had wanted for a long time to visit these historic scenes with their old castles and cathedrals which I had read about. The way the stately old buildings stirred my imagination is evident, I think, in what I wrote in my journal on May 8, the day we went to the Salisbury Cathedral: "I never thought I would hear the sound of my own feet on the ancient stone floors that had known so many famous footsteps in history." Our return voyage was on that lovely ship the *Queen Elizabeth*, and it was a perfect one with its long walks on "Prom" deck in glorious sunshine and at night a full moon marking a path of light across a placid ocean. We landed in New York on June 11.

By now I had developed the normal reaction of any author when he or she is without a writing project. As soon as one book is finished, one's interest turns to the question "What shall I write about next?"

It happened that, during my years of Lincoln research, whenever I ran across a mention of animals in connection with Lincoln, I had taken notes on the item. I thought I might some day use this interesting material. Now it occurred to me that a small book on Lincoln and animals, for children nine years old and up, might be a delightful way to introduce him to them in the warmly human role of a boy and man who loved pets. Such a book might make the great President seem like a person they had known, a person who had some of the same feelings they had.

So my next book was *Lincoln's Animal Friends*, published in 1958 and beautifully illustrated by Louis Darling. In writing it I had expert guidance from Helen Jones of Little, Brown's juvenile department. The book has no dedication as such. Instead there is a foreword beginning: "If in these pages there is some measure of understanding of Lincoln's feeling about animals, I must acknowledge my indebtedness to the pets I have loved through the years." Then follow a few brief, personaliz-

ing words about each one, from Fritzie of my little
girlhood on up to Bambi, who gave so much joy to Jim
and me in our married life.

Writing for children as young as nine required a
change of pace. Here my habit, when writing, of imagin-
ing a listener beside me to whom I am telling the story
proved very useful. I mentally seated a bright nine-year-
old child near me and the adjustment seemed to follow
naturally. It was not until a friend who had read *Lincoln's Animal Friends* said to me, "You wrote that book
for little boys," that I gave any special thought to the
fact that my imagined listener had indeed been a small
boy!

Sometimes one's readers suggest what book to write
next. A letter from a librarian told me that high-school
girls often absorb the false notions about Mrs. Lincoln
found in older volumes on Lincoln. One young matron
said in effect to this librarian, who was reviewing my
books for her group: "We all form our imperfect ideas
about Mary Lincoln in our schooldays. Why doesn't
Mrs. Randall write her story for older girls?"

I liked the idea very much. What should I call this
shorter, but equally authentic, biography? My larger
book on Mrs. Lincoln had the subtitle, *Biography of a
Marriage*. If I could use a quotation from the marriage
service, it would carry out the same idea. So the new,
smaller volume became *I Mary* as in "I Mary take thee
Abraham to my wedded husband . . ." I was unconsciously starting a series of what I would call my "I"
books.

Now the imagined listener sitting beside me as I wrote must be a high-school girl. What adjustment should I make for her age? All the high-school girls I knew were bright and keen and were reading adult books. Added to this was the fact that I always tried to write simply and clearly. So in the end I found little, if any, adjusting to do. My "I" books are for high-school age and up and my experience has been that the "and ups" respond to them in the same way the teen-agers do.

By the time *I Mary* was published, two new, wonderful friends had come into my life, Rebecca Caudill Ayars and her husband, James Sterling Ayars. Both were authors of rarely fine books for young people. In the summer of 1960 they invited me to drive with them to a workshop in juvenile literature at Appalachian State Teachers College in Boone, North Carolina. As authors, they were to be consultants, and Beulah Campbell, who conducted the workshop, had asked me to be a consultant too.

If I were writing a separate story about that blessed visit to Boone, I think I would give it the title "I *Never* Make Speeches." That was what I had been replying to the many invitations to speak which I had been receiving ever since the publication of my first book. Widowhood had increased my shyness about platforms. I agreed to go to the workshop on condition that I would not have to give a talk but would try to answer any questions that were asked me.

Under the guidance of Beulah Campbell we were soon absorbed in the activities of the workshop. Beulah had a

kind of magic in her lovely personality which set everyone to feeling at his best and wishing to join eagerly in
all endeavors.

One morning not long after our arrival I found myself
with James and Rebecca seated in front of a classroom
full of those enrolled in the workshop, mostly young
school librarians. Rebecca was first on the program and
gave a delightful talk about the writing of her books.
Then it was my turn to answer questions. The first
question was: "Tell us about the opening of the Lincoln
Papers." There was something about the situation, the
presence of Beulah and Rebecca and James, and the
eager responsiveness of the nice young audience that
made me want to talk to them. Rebecca's speech had
shown me what they wanted to know. So suddenly I
found myself making a speech without preparation or
notes, a speech fully as comprehensive as Rebecca's had
been. Beulah's eyes were sparkling and I knew James and
Rebecca were looking highly amused. Realizing the joke
was on me, I ended with a broad smile and the line: "As
you all know, I *never* make speeches!"

My next book, a biography of Colonel Elmer Ells-
worth, an interesting young man whom Lincoln loved
like a son, was published in that same year, 1960. Its
dedication reads: "To Jim, who never knew about this
book, yet helped to write it." Then I turned to another
"I" book. Mrs. Lincoln had been the First Lady of the
North during the Civil War; why not cross the lines into
Confederate territory and write about the First Lady of
the South, Mrs. Jefferson Davis? I settled down to the

long task of research and *I Varina* was published two years later. I hoped in these two "I" books I had given a close-up picture of what the Civil War meant to people living through it in both North and South.

It would be fine then if my next heroine would round things out by taking me into the wild, unsettled West as it was in the middle of the nineteenth century. Jessie Anne Benton, who married John Charles Frémont, the famous explorer of the West, proved a perfect subject. *I Jessie* was published in 1963. The following year it received in Chicago the first prize of one hundred dollars from the Friends of American Writers for the outstanding book for young people in that year. At the big award luncheon I had to make a short speech to an audience which included publishers, authors, literary critics and many other prominent people. Needless to say, in this case the speech was carefully prepared beforehand.

I have received other much-appreciated honors. About the time of my sixth book, a friend from another city said to me: "Is it true, as I hear, that you are a doctor now?" With a smile I answered, "I am four of them!" MacMurray College, Roanoke College, and Bradley University have all given me the honorary degree of Doctor of Letters or Doctor of Literature, and Knox College has conferred upon me a LL.D. degree. One of the most exciting things about getting these degrees was the distinguished company I was in. At MacMurray I took my degree along with Chief Justice Earl Warren. At Knox I was honored with Bruce

My First Honorary Degree

This picture was taken at the outdoor commencement of MacMurray College, Jacksonville, Illinois, June 6, 1954, when I received a Doctor of Literature degree. The seated gentleman, whose face is partly concealed by the railing of the platform, is Chief Justice Earl Warren.

Catton, William Hesseltine, and Allan Nevins. And at Bradley, to my great pleasure, I walked in the academic procession and took a degree with Ralph Bunche.

I Elizabeth was the fourth of my "I" books. Elizabeth, or Libbie as she was called, was the wife of General George Armstrong Custer of Custer's "last stand." While I was writing these biographies, it was as if I were living with my heroines. In one instance I had a special fellow feeling with the three of them who had met with the same problem I had. Varina Davis, Jessie Frémont, and Libbie Custer had all reached a time when they needed more money to support themselves and all three had solved the problem of financial insecurity by their writing, just as I was doing.

My work on *I Elizabeth* had had a long interruption. I had done most of the research and was writing on the first chapter when I had to take time out for eye surgery. The opacities in my eyes with which I had been born had grown into cataracts which were threatening my sight. The two operations with a long period of adjustment after each, had proved a seven months' ordeal. But Dr. E. C. Albers, who was widely known for his eye surgery, brought me through triumphantly with twenty-twenty vision, which I had never had before. It was like living through a miracle when, after so long a period of dimness and uncertainty, I reached a time when colors were dazzlingly bright, when small print, which had been a blur before, stood out with blessed distinctness, and I could read bus signs halfway down the block.

Friends as dear as one's own family had seen me through those trying seven months. When I was wheeled back to my hospital room after each operation Rebecca Ayars was waiting there to comfort me. Two couples who knew from personal experience what such eye surgery involves, Bertha and Loring Provine and Ada and Morris Leighton, kept up my courage. I have a guilty feeling that I have not done justice to all the friends who meant so much to Jim and me through the years, or to those who have been my strength and refuge since I have been alone.

Jim had told me not to seclude myself in grief after he was gone but to go out with my friends and lead a normal social life. So I had made it a rule to respond to every overture or invitation offered in friendly sympathy. The result, I think, is summed up in what an observing lady recently remarked to me. "You have more friends than almost anybody I know," she said, "and you love them all."

After the publication of *I Elizabeth*, from time to time I was asked a certain question: "When are you going to write *I Ruth?*" Long ago Allan Nevins had told me I should write a memoir of Jim. As I thought about these suggestions, I remembered that, in my speech at the award luncheon in Chicago, I had listed the qualifications the subject of my "I" books should have. The first requirement, I had said, was the existence of "intimate material, such as letters, diaries and other writings." Upon investigation I was amazed to find that, except for three years, I could, with Jim's and my diaries, give an account of each day from the time I first met him up to within three days of his death. Added to the diaries were intimate letters by the hundreds!

The second requirement read: "My leading lady must preferably have lived in the Civil War and Lincoln period." In the mental sense I knew no one who had lived more completely with the Lincolns during the Civil War than Jim and myself! The third requirement was that the lady must have married a man whose name was familiar to many. Among historians, at least, this was certainly true of Jim. It seemed to me that providence was pointing with both forefingers toward my undertaking a book called *I Ruth*.

It has been a deeply emotional experience in the past months to live my life over again in these diaries. The theme that stands out in them, through happy and unhappy events, is our devotion to each other. On our first wedding anniversary, under the stress of deep love and wartime fears, I wrote in my diary: "I thank God for the great gift of my husband, and pray for years of happiness and good together." I still thank God for Jim and the wonderful years that we shared.

As for the future, well, just the other day a literary friend said to me, "I think I have a good idea for your next book . . ."

Index